THE WORK OF ENCHANTMENT

THE WORK OF ENCHANTMENT

Matthew Del Nevo

Transaction Publishers
New Brunswick (U.S.A.) and London (U.K.)

Copyright © 2011 by Transaction Publishers, New Brunswick, New Jersey.

All rights reserved under International and Pan-American Copyright Conventions. No part of this book may be reproduced or transmitted in any form or by any means, electronic or mechanical, including photocopy, recording, or any information storage and retrieval system, without prior permission in writing from the publisher. All inquiries should be addressed to Transaction Publishers, Rutgers-The State University of New Jersey, 35 Berrue Circle, Piscataway, New Jersey 08854-8042. www.transactionpub.com

This book is printed on acid-free paper that meets the American National Standard for Permanence of Paper for Printed Library Materials.

Library of Congress Catalog Number: 2010045561
ISBN: 978-1-4128-1860-5
Printed in the United States of America

Library of Congress Cataloging-in-Publication Data

Del Nevo, Matthew.
   The work of enchantment / Matthew Del Nevo.
     p. cm.
   Includes bibliographical references and index.
   ISBN 978-1-4128-1860-5 (acid-free paper)
   1. Aesthetics. 2. Charm. I. Title.

BH301.C4D45 2011
111'.85—dc22

2010045561

There is probably no "specialist knowledge" in this area.
—*Sigmund Freud*

Contents

Preface		ix
Introduction		1
1	The Importance of Enchantment	11
2	A New Priority	21
3	"A little patch of yellow wall"	35
4	"Nothing more than a few words"	43
5	Vinteuil's Sonata	55
6	The Proper Name	61
7	Narcissus	75
8	Narcissus Later	83
9	The Turning	89
10	Dark Enchantment	95
11	"The little rust-colored sail"	103
12	The Frame of Enchantment	115

13	The Devil's Work	135
14	The Joy of Enchantment	153
Index		165

Preface

I wrote this book on freezing winter days and nights in Shanghai. I think its pages carry some of the urgency of that time and place, which is undergoing so much change and uncertainty—as we all are, whether city-bound or not.

In those chapters of this book where I discuss the writing of Marcel Proust, I have used some long quotations interwoven with my own writing. This is a stylistic device I found and liked in the work of the French philosopher Gabriel Marcel in his lectures on the German poet Rilke. The stylistic device served there to introduce the readers (or listeners, as they would have been originally) to Rilke in a substantial, first-hand way, and at the same time to provide some insight into a text which may otherwise have seemed rather arcane or difficult: Rilke is not an easy poet who you can just pick up and read and understand, without first sharing something of his sensibility. The stylistic device allows for *both* the reading of the poet (or Proust, in my case) *and* some orientation as to the sensibility required for admiration and understanding.

Introduction

This is a work about enchantment. Enchantment, today, is something we lack, something which even children miss out on, and it is in fact being extirpated from childhood by the aggressive and domineering mass-culture industries. Not just children and young people lack enchantment: so do adults. Enchantment, however, is something that the soul cannot do without, unless it is to starve. In "first-world" countries we are rich in every conceivable way, except the way of the soul, which is what this book is about. One in five people suffers mental illness in the land of plenty; but, in places where one might expect people to snap under real hardship and hopelessness, we find mental illness scarce, mental and physical obesity non-existent, and that, incredible to us, people are relatively cheerful. To the soul-starved westerner, this seems the wrong way round. A book cannot even hope to redress a cultural situation so far gone, and, anyhow, the situation is so complex that it is all but impossible to diagnose in any authoritative way. However, I am impelled to talk about enchantment.

This book is particularly about the *experience* of enchantment. Enchantment is something most of us can remember from childhood and indeed associate with that period of our lives. We find our own children enchanting, at a later stage, and then our grandchildren. However, enchantment, although perhaps the prerogative of the child, is nothing childish. Our artistic heritages are rich in enchantment and they try to teach it to us. They try to do this not by didactic methods—didactic art is bad art—but by initiating us. Art is an initiatory experience—at least, we may say this of good art, which is art that stands the test of time. Through art, as adults, we can experience enchantment in a new way that is richer than that experienced in childhood because, as adults, we are more conscious and appreciative. Art therefore gives us something, and one of the gifts it can bring—that of enchantment—is a gift of great importance. It is life enriching. Yet, we cannot experience enchantment unless we have receptive ability, and this is where culture and education come in. We stand bored and uninterested like children before artworks if we have not cultivated within ourselves the power to appreciate, to receive what great art has to give. Our approach in this book will be to cultivate and mediate the possibility of initiation present in great works of literature, picking on a very limited range. These are great because of their uncontested power of initiation, and they are of special worth when it comes to enchantment. These are works associated with the following names: Adorno, Proust, Rilke, and Goethe.

Enchantment is not a trivial subject by any stretch of the imagination. Enchantment is bound up with literature, art, philosophy, and religion—and subsidiary studies in psychology, sociology, and culture as well. I could go on. Enchantment is not for the "specialist" in any of these studies, but for everyone. The whole point of it is that it is quintessentially human. The trouble is that most of us lose touch with it after a certain age, so it is consigned to children's books; and we imagine art has to do with something else. But of course when we look at a lot of contemporary art, it often *does* have to do with something else. Art is sick. Culture is sick too. When art has lost its charm, even a perverse charm but a charm nonetheless, it is sick. In a culture where "charm" is an archaic word which no one uses—and other more commercially viable values take its place—and where codes of practice replace manners, culture is not well either. But of course art and culture interplay and feed off each other. This is where critical theory comes in: it "critiques" this situation, unmasking it, trying to revolutionize it, ultimately for the good, if that is possible. At the center of this critique (if we may call it that), is not a new theory, but a defense of the humanities, of philosophy, religion, art and, in this book, of *beauty*, as the major criterion of the true and the good.

Enchantment, essentially, is the possibility of being captivated by the beautiful. But this is because *enchantment is the desire of the soul*.

But before we can be captivated, we must *recapture* the experience of enchantment; this is what this book is trying to enable us to do. Enchantment should be an essential part of our story—not the missing ingredient of life. Enchantment is what raises our life out of the mere drudgery of "existence." Enchantment is *beyond* the mere definition of the word. Enchantment, as "being captivated by the beautiful," *deliberately* defers the meaning. But this does not worry us. What we have in this book is a movement from start to finish, from beginning to end, in various stages (chapters), in which enchantment is held before us indirectly. This is the only way to approach it.

The medieval Jewish philosopher Maimonides wrote a famous and now classic work of religious philosophy called *Guide for the Perplexed*. All religion could be said to be a guide for the perplexed of some kind or another. The "consolations of religion" (or of philosophy, for that matter) refer to the capacity of religion (or of philosophy) to put an end to perplexity and provide the comfort that answers give in the form of beliefs and accompanying ways of life and community. However, it also remains true that every worthwhile perspective is a site of perplexity; otherwise, it merely spells ideology and dogmatism. For many of us, religious beliefs (or philosophies) raise more questions than they answer—and this is no bad thing. Questions will lead more readily to enchantment—enchantment, you see, gives rise to them!—than answers. Unphilosophical, "artless," or unreflective religion displaces enchantment in the sphere of the spirit as readily as does commodity capitalism in the material sphere. I will have more to say on this later. Enchantment is not a subject that can be enclosed, fixed, or fixated in ready-made one-size-fits-all answers without destroying its magic, which is always the magic of a moment. That is why I did not define enchantment earlier, but deferred to beauty. It is also why, in following the movement of the showing in this book, I will be suggestive, rather than conclusive. My purpose is to orient my reader, not enchant him/her. It is art—not the commentary on it—that exists for enchantment.

Enchantment in an artwork has something to do with being partly in another world while still in this one. What I have called "the work" of enchantment—by which I mean the activity that leads us to it and trains us for it, namely, reading, listening, and gazing—is our way of access to this other world while still in this one. The "other" world, of enchantment, accessed through the work of enchantment, enriches this. We instantly feel this "other" world, as we shall, shortly, when I will quote the French novelist Marcel Proust, writing in the first quarter of the twentieth century, just a few lines, but instantly we feel his world and it enters ours. Every world that enters ours affects it, to enchant it or otherwise. Reading, listening, and gazing are then of enormous importance as acts which have the capacity to change our lives into "enchanted lives," in the real sense, not the kitsch sense, and the difference will emerge through these pages gradually as I will endeavor to provide the ability to discern the difference.

As I hinted already, our contemporary culture is not one that naturally lends itself to enchantment. Our "developed" society, as we call it—in contrast to "developing" societies, which presumably want to be like us, at least with regard to wealth and capital—is a hectic, active, competitive society that "never stops," as we sometimes boast. The philosophy that governs such a society, which is unwittingly present in the way we do things, the way we see things (and given in what we do not do and do not see as well), is the philosophy of pragmatism. This, in a nutshell, is the "can-do" philosophy, which, while it started from the United States and is most strongly associated with Americans (according to the sociologist Max Weber [1864–1920] in his now classic study, which links the Protestant ethic with the spirit of capitalism[1]), takes us back before the founding of America. Of course this "Protestant ethic," by which Weber means the work ethic essentially (and the purely business-minded mentality), was born in Europe and only exported from there to America. In any case, it is true to say that pragmatism is inherently utilitarian, that is, it consists in an attitude where the means do not always justify the end, but, if it makes most people happy, then these means surely do. Pragmatism, at the same time, puts a premium on individual liberty. The individual is (seemingly, anyway) released to "get on with it" and make themselves happy in whatever way works for them; and it is therefore "up to them," as we say. If the individual's happiness is too much at the expense of others, it can be problematic; at the same time, the unhappiness of others is often invisible, because it is in the interests of those who are most successful at carving out their "careers" to keep it this way—and it is also within their power to do so. Of course, a basic moral code prevails, under-girding the pragmatism, more or less—a moral code relating to happiness as people discover, for themselves, what Aristotle said long ago, namely, that it is impossible to be happy and immoral: the two just do not equate. People make this discovery for themselves, one generation after the next.

Weber used the word "disenchantment" in an essay on the practice of science and it became a coinage associated with his thought—one, in fact, fundamental to it. Science explains the world to us by quantifying the world and intellectualizing the results of these quantifications. Weber argued that quite different cultures know the world the way they know it, differently from us, and they may even know it better. For example, a traditional man may know his tools, whereas we do not know our fridges, computers, cars, and so on; we know only how to use them. We have the feeling that, if we wanted to, we *could* know about these things because both our tools and the world to which they belong are all ordered and planned. We live in a world of total calculation which allows us to say we *could* know about x or y if we wanted. But this possibility does not really make us any more knowing *in fact*. The Anglo-Celtic Australian knows less about the outback when it comes down to it than the Aborigine, although we can mine it, measure it, and so on. "The increasing rationalization and intellectualization do not, therefore, indicate an increased general knowledge of the conditions under which one lives."[2] Science—this calculative mode of being in the world and experiencing the world—pushes out non-scientific explanations, spiritual or philosophical or religious explanations, and this, says Weber, "means that the world is disenchanted." In a society which is basically a planned economy, reading, listening, and gazing come to be about technical matters "that count." In this way reading, listening, and gazing are themselves disenchanted and part of the "work ethic."

I am saying all this, sketchily, in order to make the point that, in our developed society, reading, listening, and gazing, as part of the work of the arts and humanities, go by the board; they get pushed to the side as incidental, something to do when you have "got time," or to "pass the time," or when you have not got something "more important to do." The words I put in double quotes here (and often elsewhere) do not mean to be ironic, but to capture expressions and attitudes in words that govern us from the inside out; yet they are words that reflect values we hold most strongly, even if we do not know we hold them. Learning to read is important if we are to "get on" in life, in a competitive can-do world—and to swim, not sink; but this is not the reading I am talking about. Reading signposts, instruction manuals, and internet sites is not the kind of reading I mean. What I mean by reading is best given by Marcel Proust in his little essay "Days of Reading."[3] The author is sure that he has never spent days more fully than those he spent with a favorite book. Everything else, which most people considered important, "I pushed aside as a vulgar impediment to a heavenly pleasure."[4]

I do not doubt that this whole book is hardly more than an expansion on that line by Proust.

Most people would think of reading in the same way as young Marcel's Great Aunt Léonie in Proust's novel *Remembrance of Things Past*:

> While I read in the garden, something my great-aunt would not have understood my doing except on Sunday, a day when it was forbidden to occupy oneself with anything serious and when she did not sew (on a weekday she would have said to me, "What? Still *amusing* yourself with a book? This isn't Sunday, you know," giving the word amusement the meaning of childishness and waste of time)...[5]

Here, reading is creative soul-work, done half in secret. It looks passive and ordinary enough, from the outside, to Aunt Léonie, but to the one reading, from the point of view of the inside, the reader exists in another time, not the time of clocks, but the time of the soul and the slow time—or "timelessness"—of soulfulness, in which one is filled with other life, garnered from the pages of a book. Such reading is "psychoanalytical" in the proper sense of an activity that sorts through our thoughts and feelings, unraveling and unknotting our imagination and our soul—if the book is worth reading. In a book, that other world, of which the pages tell, enters our world; but first we must pick up and read (*tolle lege*). A book can be a dangerous prospect, an exciting prospect, a wonderful prospect, and an enchanting prospect. Here, a book is more like Kafka's idea of a book as "an axe for the frozen sea inside us," something that stirs us up and is fundamentally transformative. Reading that not only fills our days to the brim, but changes our outlook and our prospects.

Listening, too, is transformative. Listening is something we do all the time; it is central to functioning in society and keeping up with it. But this is not the sort of listening I mean. We can hear something but not have really *listened*. One philosopher, Jean-Luc Nancy, has said that in our culture "listening" has too often, and wrongly, been collapsed into the meaning of "understanding." But listening has its own *touch*, which is not the *grasp* of understanding. Listening can "let be" *as is*, rather than "take in" and consume by "understanding." To understand is to turn what is listened to into words, perhaps on a page, without a sound in their printed form, or into sound which is completely and utterly different, if spoken, from what was listened to at first. Listening takes time and training, just as developing "a musical ear" or a sense of timing does. To listen is not just to "tune in" to whatever it is and get on the "same wavelength," but more seriously, for enchantment, listening is an *attunement* with what is essentially other; it is not the same as the words we might translate this other into in speech or writing. Listening is a way of *receiving*.

Gazing too is transformative. At school we were told by the teacher not to gaze out the window or into space, but to "pay attention." We went on school trips to museums or art galleries and there we were permitted to gaze at what we liked. Today some people spend massive amounts of time watching television or computer screens, but none of this is proper gazing. Gazing is an *absorption*. To gaze is to absorb oneself or be absorbed by what one is looking at; one can "see" and "look," but not, in our sense, gaze. Gazing needs one's *time* absorbed in it, so that you forget time and the time you spent gazing becomes another time without space. Gazing absorbs your being, and time vanishes into the gaze. But gazing is not gawping or staring (as at a screen); with a gaze, a true gaze as we mean it here, our sensibility is being nourished and elevated; at something which is merely entertaining (although it might be absorbing in some sense too) we do not "gaze," rather we are "taken in" by it. In gazing we are not "taken in" but between my gaze and that at which I gaze, the distance is infinite, however intimate the moment. This is the wonder of gazing.

Lastly, by way of introduction, while I am aware of other books on enchantment, for instance the work of Bruno Bettelheim, which I esteem (despite the posthumous controversy about his political incorrectness), and works by others (who will remain unmentioned by name) because I am in fundamental disagreement with either their New Age view of enchantment, or their ideological view which wants "re-enchantment," thereby tying enchantment to a pragmatic project. This book is not about such other books. In every chapter that follows, I go to *the matter itself*: enchantment. This is my method, which, in philosophy, is called "phenomenological." However, I have not followed the jargon of philosophical phenomenology, or invented my own new jargon to replace it; rather, I am following the older "ordinary language" tradition which really goes right back to Aristotle and upholds a fundamentally truth-bearing ordinary language, where it already exists, or works philosophically for it, where it does not. This is my approach. For this reason, I have approached enchantment through literature, which of course is written in ordinary language at a popular, or at least at an optimally communicative, level. While most of this book is taken up with discussion of extracts from works of Proust, Rilke, and Goethe, the book is not about them (or, more precisely, their works), and neither is enchantment, of course. Rather, Proust, Rilke, and Goethe have *iconic* status, in that it will be through their words, as through windows, that we will be able to learn what this work of enchantment is all about. It is an indirect and non-theoretical approach. This is my method. Therefore, my "theory" of enchantment, such as it is, will be suggestive, rather than stipulatory and dogmatic. The work of enchantment ultimately lies with us; enchantment must start with our own work of reading, listening, and gazing; and this work is never a mere matter of "getting the information" or "having the low-down." Enchantment is a philosophy of life and it is a *kind* of life; in this book it is the kind of life in which art plays a significant role. We come to enchantment through art, and we come to art through the work of enchantment: reading, listening, and gazing.

Notes

1. Max Weber, *The Protestant Ethic and the 'Spirit' of Capitalism* (1905), trans. Peter Baehr (London: Penguin, 2002).
2. Weber, "Science as a Vocation," in *Essays in Sociology* (1922), ed. H.H. Gerth & C. Wright Mills (London: Routledge, 1970), 139.
3. Marcel Proust, "Days of Reading," in *Against Sainte-Beuve*, trans. John Sturrock (London: Penguin, 1988), 195–233.
4. Ibid., 195.
5. Proust, *In Search of Lost Time*, Volume 1, trans. Lydia Davis (London: Penguin, 2003), 102.

1

The Importance of Enchantment

In this chapter and the next, I will sketch out, very broadly, the main philosophical parameters or framework in which the work of enchantment is to take place—this is like, in gardening, preparing the soil, or, in cooking, getting the pans and implements ready. First we need to appreciate the importance of enchantment, which has to do with our cultural context in which the work of enchantment takes place; then we need to appreciate what I have called "the new priority," which is about our historical position "after the war." Here I will refer by "the war" to the two World Wars that took up the better part of the first half of the twentieth century and that continues to spill over and break out in other places, right into today. We are conscious of war and peace in a new way which is historically unprecedented.

In the Introduction I said that enchantment is something the soul cannot do without unless it is to starve. This is not just a metaphor. There is a question: with what are we feeding our inner world? This is the most important psychological question of health and wellbeing, because we can actually destroy ourselves without even realizing it by feeding our inner world with rubbish. People can "die inwardly" even before they are dead physically. The idea of the "living dead" is not just a horror movie: it can be a psychological reality—although, of course, because our humanity cannot be erased, the dead (in this sense) can be brought back to life. There is no better tonic for the soul than enchantment. But enchantment does not just happen: one must be ready for it.

Adorno, Proust, Lou Salomé, Rilke, and Goethe are important names for enchantment. While all of these writers, except Adorno, wrote creative literature (novels or poetry), and while we will be greatly concerned with fiction, we should not imagine that enchantment is therefore "fictitious." What do "fiction" and "non-fiction" indicate, anyway, when it comes to enchantment? Our imagination interferes with reality, in either case, transforming and deforming it, whatever "it"—reality—truly is. Adorno, Proust, Salomé, Rilke, and Goethe—whoever these people really were we will never know. And not knowing is important to enchantment because it knows that some things, sometimes the most precious things, are kept secret, or that secrecy surrounds them, and love and wisdom, philosophy that is, are full of secrets and words that have been whispered.

It is significant that, while we cannot know Adorno or Proust or the others like they knew themselves, how well did they know themselves? How well do I know myself?—or you, my reader? The truth is that we can never become objects to ourselves in experience. "Know Thyself," the old philosophical adage, is a chimera. There are no objective measures of the soul. But we need to realize that there are no subjective measures either! And yet, judgments are possible. They are made possible on the basis of the works of art and literature that enchant us and by which we take our measure of who we are, who we have become, and who we want to turn out to be like.

Adorno sets the philosophical coordinates in this book. He studied music in Vienna with Alban Berg and became an accomplished musician and musicologist. Adorno also wrote one of the best philosophical works of the twentieth century, *Aesthetic Theory* (1970). He is a famously difficult writer, but we should not be put off by his reputation; in any case, we will not need to go deeply into his thinking for its own sake, but just enough to derive some sensible orientation for our understanding of the work of enchantment.

We need to appreciate (and this is what Adorno will clearly show us) that enchantment is not the same at all times and in all places. In this book we want to see what enchantment means for us in "advanced" or "developed" countries today—and, negatively, what the social disablement of enchantment means too.

There is therefore a social and critical side to my account. One cannot speak of enchantment, if one is to speak of it with any worth or validity, in isolation from the social and political milieu in which it is to exist, or which resists its existence. I will just add an introductory comment about this now, before we proceed. Just as commodity capitalism can never be green in the sense of supporting locales into which it reaches—simply because an earth-friendly economics would have to be highly socially responsive and responsible and therefore not "free"—neither can this kind of irresponsible and irresponsive capitalism *bring enchantment*. "Big" capitalism, as I call it, where self-interest, development, sales, consumption, profit margins, and financial reporting are all that really count, and where money is the "bottom line," provides the *simulacra* of enchantment with an infinite array of entertainments, gimmicks, and distractions, nearly all of which require money. Big capitalism provides delusory substitutes for enchantment, for instance, the *glamour* that surrounds things instead of the *aura* of enchantment. Glamour is generated by a massive advertising industry driving almost everything—even, today, the news, although that particular product is by definition not supposed to be glamorous, which is precisely its glamour. Even violence and gambling are made out to be glamorous. The point is that glamour in our age stands in (more and more) for enchantment, but my argument is that big capitalism can never provide enchantment, only the fake substitute. Many we call "celebrities" lead glamorous lives which, very often, are totally disenchanted, but so many young people, pathetically, aspire to "be like that"; and of course they learn this attitude from adults who do not know better.

Big capitalism produces a consumer culture and in this culture even culture itself becomes industrialized, glamorized, and cultural items become things and commodities which, in a sense, steal their charm and their reality—this, following Adorno, we call "the culture industry." These "culture industries" (using the plural so as not to lump them together as one undifferentiated entity)—and we know their brand names—are more and more decisive for children and young adults regarding their "likes," "dislikes," and general interests.

The culture industries suck cultural capital out of society. Cultural capital, a term of sociologist Pierre Bourdieu, is what has gone to "make" a culture and is therefore constitutive of it—even psychologically. Cultural capital is human *creation* accumulated over the centuries and despite wars, but, in our time, the culture industries replace it (for the most part anyway) with junk entertainments and leave the shell. It is increasingly difficult for enchantment to survive in this atmosphere, up against the superpowers of the culture industries that tear it down and destroy it. My point here is merely that, in my story of enchantment, the social critical edges of the subject will be evident, and in fact they are crucial to any account of the subject.

Adorno was an arch critic of big capitalism and big socialism, and no fan of popular culture. Proust, Rilke, and Goethe knew little or nothing about popular culture compared to ourselves, and the little they did know they tended to see as vulgarism. However, my own stance is that enchantment is possible in popular culture, as, I imagine, it is in any culture. For, simply, where there are human beings there is creativity, and where there is creativity there can be enchantment—and popular culture is no exception to this fact. Nevertheless, it is more difficult to grasp enchantment, as we need to, *first and foremost* through examples of popular culture. Proust, Rilke, and Goethe will give us easier access to the subject of enchantment. Then, with a sense of enchantment, and the work of enchantment, we will be able to think about popular culture in a more informed way. With the demise of the humanities within schools and higher education the importance of reading, listening, and gazing as ways, within individuals, of building cultural capital which later on will play out in society and snowball over time, there is hardly anyone left any longer who can explain things as naturally and easily as we find them in Proust, Rilke, and Goethe. This is why I am dipping into their writings.

Despite the culture industries, I *do* believe that creative individuals and teams of people are able to stand clear of it. The culture industries by no means control creativity, nor, I believe, can they contain it. A good example is the film director—and there are many great artists among them—Chaplin, Hitchcock, Pasolini, Kazan, Rohmer, and living names like Mike Leigh, Roman Polanski, Chen Kaige, and

Zhang Yimou. Film directors' artistic talents are never contained and controlled (totalized) by the film culture industry. Chaplin, wrote, directed, and starred in *The Kid*, even writing the musical score, and no amount of money or technological innovation can ever replace the startling genius—the truly human element—evident in a film like that. More often, of course, the director works through his or her actors and these are mediated through a huge number of differentials, such as editing or casting. But a great director will oversee the differentials. The film will be his or her work—Agnes Varda would do her own editing. The great director will and does outstrip the tendency to the complete commercialization of the genre in order to make the film an artwork. Sad then that so few films may be considered works of art as they are completely commercially oriented and therefore only industrial outputs.

Even when genres seem to belong wholesale to the culture industry, and to be most obviously industrial outputs, such as "pop" and "rap," even then new talent can arise which is real artistic talent, in the sense we cover it in this book, to shake the industry. Take, for example, the guitarist, drummer, songwriter, and band leader Jack White, who is reinventing the raw voice and stomping boots of blues man Sun House in another century; or take the example of the entertainer and actor Tom Waits or, at the other end of the spectrum, pianist and singer-songwriter Tori Amos. Indie music is by definition made and performed outside or over and against the commercial industrialization of rock music, and while it may venture into the market to make money, to survive, its roots are not there.

And consumers are not *just* consumers. Many consumers are not just horrid "culture-vultures" or passive "couch potatoes," but actually have the "savvy" to recognize the creative edge; this is enough to keep the culture industries themselves from complacency or even from ceasing to strive after "the shock of the new." In this sense, therefore, the culture industries do not just manufacture their product, but *also* they are *in harness* with really creative individuals and teams of people. Between the monopolizing power of the culture industries and the unique power of creative individuals, there is a relationship in which the latter continues to surpass, escape, and remain "outside" the system constituted by the former. For example, Kat von D would be Kat von D with or without television. She is soulful in the sense meant in this book; and only after that is she a television "star" or "media personality." Of course, at a certain point of "fame," this dynamic becomes confused, which is one of the problems of fame and why it can indirectly, as a result of the "pressure," break and destroy "stars" as well.

By naming names from popular culture, as I have just done, one immediately faces the trouble that these names also indicate judgments of taste that someone else or even everyone else can easily disagree with and, therefore, disagree with everything else I have got to say. If we want to understand the work of enchantment, or what it can mean for a woman to be an enchantress, it is better to go back to Rilke and Lou Salomé, as we shall. Once we have established with their help what we mean, it will be much easier to see it in the popular sphere. This then is our tactic.

Let us not blame big capitalism and the culture industries alone for disenchantment: *religion* can kill enchantment just as well as glamour. Religious pomp, on one hand, and religious Puritanism, on the other, are both inimical for enchantment and therefore for the soul. The trouble is that a person can be very religious but totally soulless. Not much theology at all attends to this problem, but it can be a real problem in real communities. By religious "pomp" I mean retrograde ritualism, ritual pietism—even reification and fetishism under the guise of "holiness"; and by "Puritanism" I mean the stripping back of all the "trappings" from religion. Both opposed tendencies, which, possibly, may make us very spiritual in the eyes of others, are soul-destroying; and I cannot see how what is soul-destroying can be good for the spirit.

Reason, I believe, is the precondition for enchantment, as it is for religion that is not superstitious and not the religiosity or sanctimony by which people vainly delude themselves in the name of revelation. However, having said this, religion is hierarchical and works at different levels with different sorts of people, and so what might *not* be misleading at one level may *seem* to be so at another level; but this is all merely relative, and, overall, reason may be said to be in play throughout: from pure simplicity to the heights and depths of erudition. Among the achievements of the Italian

Renaissance, which influences me, is the discovery of the experimental and properly scientific spirit, and, correspondingly, the discovery of nature, nostalgia for the past and for cultural memory, and along with these, the pursuit of scientific *research*.

Scientific thinking and poetic thinking are surprisingly harmonized by the work of enchantment. They are harmonized in two ways: in the nature of what we mean by "thinking," and educationally. On this latter point—education—the philosopher Wittgenstein, in 1939, wrote of a situation that has since got worse: "People nowadays think that scientists exist to instruct them, poets, musicians etc. to give them pleasure. The idea *that these have something to teach them*—that does not occur to them."[1] An educative quality is one thing the sciences and the arts have in common. Education does not just "inform" us, as a lot of people mistakenly think about education; it "educes," that is, it calls us into our personal potential, collectively, over time. Education forms culture.

"Scientific thought is, in its essence, no different from the normal processes of thinking which we all, *believers and unbelievers alike*, make use of when we are going about our business in everyday life." So said Freud in 1933.[2] "It [scientific thought] has merely taken a special form in certain respects: it extends its interest to things which have no immediately obvious utility, it endeavors to eliminate personal factors and emotional influences, it carefully examines the trustworthiness of the sense perceptions which are not obtainable by everyday means, and isolates the determinates of these new experiences by purposely varied experimentation. Its aim is to arrive at correspondence with reality."[3]

The work of enchantment is not an escape from reality, but faces the truth of reality. Freud's science was psychoanalysis, which, in the words of Thomas Mann, confronts "the mysterious unity of the ego and actuality, destiny and character, doing and happening." We follow the genius of Thomas Mann in believing that there is a profound sympathy between psychoanalysis and creative literature or poetry: the one investigates the soul, the other gives expression to it as art.

To get into the work of enchantment, we need a scientific sensibility as described by Freud (which differs from the non-humanist definition of science in terms of methodology and technology), but we also need art and artistic sensibility. Poetic thought (taken in the broad sense) and art are imaginative. "The imagination is regulated by art, especially by poetry. There is nothing more frightful than imagination without taste." So said Goethe in 1821.[4] Scientific thought will correspond to the external world within the bounds of bare reason—and imagination will clothe bare reason within the bounds of the ethical sense written on our hearts—if imagination is to be tasteful, or, as we will say, soul-making. Our inner freedom is the precondition for soul-making, as it is for moral responsibility; but these are merely fine words and, without the work of enchantment making light of them, they become the prerogatives of the sanctimonious and moralistic.

Poetic thinking too has its reasons. Scientific thought, properly conceived, and poetic thought, also properly conceived, need not be contraries. In these pages they are woven together.

"The relationship of the arts and sciences to life is very different, depending on the level at which they are situated, on the conditions of the time, and on thousands of other chance factors. For this reason no one can easily make sense of the whole." So wrote Goethe.[5]

Many before and since Goethe have deluded themselves (and others) that they could make sense of the whole, but enchantment of the soul is infinite and the only absolute is in the individual case. And yet the intention that seeks to make the incomprehensible comprehensible is honorable in itself.

Working within these parameters for sane and sociable thinking, "we all, believers and unbelievers alike" will find in the story about enchantment that follows important clues toward a philosophy of life, especially with regard to the fulfillment or frustration of our desires; and I hope we will see, in no uncertain terms, the importance of enchantment.

Notes

1. Ludwig Wittgenstein, *Culture and Value*, ed. G.H. von Wright, trans. Peter Winch (Chicago: University of Chicago Press, 1984), 36e.
2. Sigmund Freud, "On the Question of a *Weltanschauung*" (1933), in *An Outline of Psychoanalysis*, trans. Helena Ragg-Kirkby (London: Penguin, 2003), 159. (Italics added to original)

3. Thomas Mann, "Freud and the Future," in *Essays of Three Decades*, trans. H.T. Lowe-Porter (London: Secker & Warburg, 1946), 411–12.
4. Johann Wolfgang von Goethe, "Reflections in the Spirit of the Wanderers," in *Wilhelm Meister's Journeyman Years or The Renunciants. Goethe's Collected Works*, Volume 10, trans. Jan van Heurck, Krishna Winston (New York: Suhrkamp, 1989), 301. (Henceforth: *Journeyman Years*)
5. Ibid., 299.

2

A New Priority

The new priority I talk about in this chapter has to do with our historical position "after the war," by which I mean primarily the Second World War and its aftermath, although the roots of the Second World War were the First World War, and the roots of that were the breakdown—the complete meltdown—of Christian culture in Europe that had been slowly gathering pace during the nineteenth century. This meltdown is evident if we read the works of ideas; the philosophy of Hegel and Schopenhauer in the first half of the nineteenth century already assumes their era is post-Christian. It is the era of the Enlightenment, the era after Kant, who completely revolutionized philosophy; and this is not the era it was before. The meltdown of Christian culture in Europe in the nineteenth century within philosophy reaches its culmination, perhaps, in the work of Nietzsche, who wants, quite dramatically, to have done with it. He masqueraded himself in one of his last books, before he descended into madness, as the Anti-Christ, which is the book's title. But other writers, such as Dostoevsky and Soloviov, were seeing and saying something similar while imagining a transformation of Christianity. If there is a transformation of Christianity in the twentieth century, particularly after the Jewish Holocaust, then it is on the terms given by the Enlightenment and the secular age, not by ages past.

I will only be sketching some of the main lines, as I see them, of this historical situation here. It is a large and immensely complex subject. We do not need to get embroiled in it for the purposes of appreciating the work of enchantment, but we do need to grasp one or two basic truths of a time such as ours. Perhaps the truth is that enchantment is difficult in a technological age, whereas it is easy for people to become adjuncts of technology. Machines, even those new devices which we do not regard any more as machines but almost as extensions of ourselves, because we love them so much and use them continually and hold them almost all day long, or at least "have them on," even these machines, basically speaking, are just tools. Tools for communication, or pleasure perhaps. In an age of technology it is easy for these things to dominate our lives and we then become adjuncts of technology; we become the unwitting tools of our own tools. This is one of the matters we need to be aware of and that I will make some further deliberately sketchy (but not hasty) points about. Another basic truth of a time such as ours might be the difficulty of making good art, since everything is turned by business into a commodity or product. The point is that the complete domination of art by business, which is typical of our time and place in history, makes it hard for art to operate as a basis for the work of enchantment as it once did—even in the days of Proust, Rilke, and Goethe, who I will talk about later. Sketching out these basic truths just a little further is the substance of what follows in this chapter; again, I have tended to be suggestive, appealing to my reader's "common sense," rather than to theoretical and imposing, conclusive views that I hold. Obviously, everything I say is open to discussion on every side.

These words strike me as important for us who desire to appreciate the work of enchantment: "The *inner life*: one is almost ashamed to pronounce this pathetic expression in the face of so many realisms and objectivisms."[1]—from 1966, the ironically intended words of Emmanuel Levinas, Jewish philosopher, Holocaust survivor. But then he said we must give *new priority to the inner life*. We need to give new priority to the inner life because of the realisms and objectivisms which hem us in on all sides, and indeed, which we internalize and which become our beliefs, dogmas, and ideologies. Before we enter into this conflict that Levinas suggests we are inextricably part of—the conflict between our inner life and the ostensible realisms and objectivisms that stand over and against it, blocking it, perhaps—I shall clarify a couple of proper names belonging to the inner life of these pages: "soul" and "enchantment."

"Soul" is a word that refers to the unity, or more precisely, unison, of our inner sensibilities and sensitivities. Soul-working, therefore, refers to inner work or inner development, the kinds of activities we involve ourselves in or the attitude we take to those activities that will strengthen that unison and at the same time deepen that inner sensibility and sensitivity. Soul-working is characteristically reflective, and the kind of work that best suits soul-making is constitutive of those disciplines that used to be known, at least within the university, as "the humanities." This is the work of reading, of listening and of gazing. It is a question today, in our "now" culture of instant gratifications and fixes, of how to do such work. I passed the literacy test, but can I really *read* in the true sense of the word? For instance, as we shall see in what follows, reading a newspaper does not count at all as reading in a way that is soul-making. Quite a lot of what passes for reading today fails this test, and is not really reading except in a trivial sense. Something similar may be said of the other two modes of soul-working: listening and gazing. Am I able really *to listen*? Am I able really *to gaze* at something properly? Culture requires that we be capable of reading, listening, and gazing. There is no real culture where these are absent; perhaps, instead, there is merely commerce or simply ignorance.

"Soul" is not a thing I have. I do not "have" a soul. I am one. But I may not be if I do no soul-work—and let me say, lest this sound snobbish, or elitist, which it is not meant to be: everyone who listens to children is doing soul-work. Mothers are the outstanding representatives of what I am talking about. And grandparents. Above all, teachers. Fathers?—wherever they are present to their children. More generally, all *people who care* qualify, which really should be everyone. We are all of us *souls* as the essence of our human being. Soul is what I am: *I am* this inner unison of sensibility and sensitivity. When someone lacks this quality in their persona, we ordinarily call them "unimaginative." If a person is chronically unimaginative we call them a "psychopath"; we actually consider them seriously sick. Soul, therefore, is still important. We still need to "save our souls," which is really what I am calling soul-work or soul-making (I use the two terms interchangeably).

But although soul is quintessentially human, and what I am, we live more and more in a soulless world in which inner sensibility and sensitivity is sullied and stultified and dehumanized: consider the priority of money-making, to take one example, and the consequent exploitation of everything imaginable for commercial ends, especially sex, violence, vanity, and selfishness. What we call "globalization" is actually—even mainly—the globalization of these things. The globalization of human rights (our one and only check, and a poor one at that) follows in train to stem "abuses." But for those with eyes to see, it is a pathetic and nearly neo-barbaric scenario. At a more "micro" level, to take another example, consider children glued to computer games. These are not really "games" in a proper sense: we have forgotten what a game really is. There are young adults who have no idea what I could possibly mean by referring to "what a game really is." I know children who cannot play anymore unless plugged into these pre-set gadgets, which conceptually and intellectually are extremely primitive. Children cannot play because they have got no imagination. They find reading, listening, and gazing hard because they lack imagination. This is alarming, but no one is much alarmed. Our schools do a wonderful job at turning back the tide, and, to my mind, teachers are the heroes of our culture—what is left of it.

"Enchantment," the second notion I wish to clarify, is what the soul wants: it is what feeds the soul—and our soul should be hungry. The thing is, with the soul, because it is the same as myself, I can lose it without noticing it. I mean I can lose that inner sensibility and sensitivity. It can vanish like ozone. The philosopher Søren Kierkegaard wrote in 1849: "The biggest danger, that of losing oneself, can pass off in the world as quietly as if it were nothing; every other loss, an arm, a leg, five dollars, a wife, etc. is bound to be noticed."[2] Because soul refers to the unity of inner sensitivity and inner sensibility, if we lose this we have lost the capacity to notice the loss; and if we live among like-minded people, they would not notice it either. Life can disappear from our midst with no one noticing and no one taking it from us. This is the human condition. But this is where the humanities, which I mentioned before, come in. Our weapons against the psychopathic forces driving the de-souling of the world are reading, listening, and gazing. Science and technology cannot help; indeed, they are much too much part of the problem already. Reading, listening, and gazing, to our deafened ears, do not sound like much; they sound weak and possibly a waste of time. But, actually, by these alone can we save our souls. By these alone can we resurrect the traditional power of education, ethics, and politics. The solution to so many of our problems lie in these paltry activities. They disarm so many people I talk to because they are not theories. People believe in theories and are even desperate for them—and dogmatic about them when they get possessed by one they believe in. But reading, listening, and gazing are not theories any more than gardening or cooking or raising children are. However, so many people have lost a sense of reading, gazing, and listening as soul-making, whereas gardening, cooking, and raising children, because they are more obviously practical and seemingly more necessary, continue to attract attention and enthusiasm, and continue to be soul-making. Yet, for soul, the less practical pursuits provide the more powerful way.

Enchantment is what the soul needs and what this book is about. Enchantment is what reading, listening, and gazing ultimately reward us with. The enchantment which starts on the inside of us will be externalized over time, in the passage from past to future. The world we will build together will start within us. If our inner sensitivity and sensibility—our faculty of imagination principally, we might say—is enriched, then the world we build together will be the richer for it. Dullards and psychopaths, when they rule the world, will never create a just and livable order. We recreate on the outside what (psychologically speaking) is within; we cannot do otherwise. And what is within us will objectify itself over the generations; it cannot do otherwise. The inner work of enchantment, then, is essential to *humanity* in the best and fullest sense of that concept. If you want a title for my "theory" in the pages that follow, it is no theory and has no method: it is a philosophy of culture and art. Reading, listening, and gazing have to do with what we cultivate and how we cultivate it. Art has to do with the expression or "shape" we give to reading, listening, and gazing, which, while it always has to do with words and is wrapped up in them, is beyond them and not reducible to them.

Now, coming back to that quotation we started with, as Emmanuel Levinas had said: "The *inner life*: one is almost ashamed to pronounce this pathetic expression in the face of so many realisms and objectivisms." If this is so, then the stakes of this book are high. For a start, the very notion of "enchantment" has been co-opted by fairytales for children (although there is nothing wrong with that), fantasy, and, more dubiously, spiritualities—New Age, Jungian, Celtic, Mythic, Gnostic, Hermetic, Alternative, and so on. Enchantment has been lost from the humanities, where it really belongs. However, the humanities today have largely been put out of the university, where they were once the heart and soul, and have been replaced by science and training. Now, such theoretical and method-based disciplines certainly have a place around the humanities, but they should not replace them, as they have; rather, they should feed into them.

But the humanities have a further problem, and that is their historical nature. The humanities—whatever the term might mean today, and assuming it is still legitimate and meaningful to speak of them—are not the same now as before the catastrophic breakdown of European culture in the first half of the twentieth century. It has been since 1945, and especially since the late 1960s, with the rise of all sorts of *nouveau* sciences and pseudo-subject-areas, that the humanities have not found their feet, as it were; and this is understandable. If we are going to present enchantment as intrinsic to the existence of the humanities and of subsequent culture worthy of the name, then it is from our historical position that we do this; and it is neither, as we shall see, "reactionary" nor "conservative" to do so, it is not even essentially political. We can still speak of enchantment, I believe, because reading, listening, and gazing are pursuits which anyone can engage in, and because these pursuits belong not only to our experience as adults but also within educational settings at all levels. Further, my experience within educational settings encourages me in the belief that we can still speak of enchantment—that it is not "a thing of the past"—because almost invariably people ("the public" or students) are glad to discover a pathway (reading, listening, gazing) that will be enchanting, and that they would never thereafter give up, because it is beautiful and soul-enriching. But that is where the pathway leads, not where it starts.

The antithesis of believing enchantment to be possible or even desirable would seem to be made by Adorno's well-worn statement of 1949: "To write poetry after Auschwitz is barbaric."[3] In his 1965 Lectures on Metaphysics, Adorno said that his statement that "after Auschwitz one could no longer write poetry...gave rise to a discussion I did not anticipate when I wrote those words."[4] He says he meant "to point to the hollowness of the resurrected culture of that time—it could equally well be said, that one *must* write poems, in keeping with Hegel's statement in the *Aesthetics*, that as long as there is an awareness of suffering among human beings *there must also be art as the objective form of that awareness*."[5] (Paul Celan's and Edmond Jabès' poetry, for instance. Both wrote exemplary poetry after Auschwitz—even about it.) But Adorno's own philosophy—these very lectures on metaphysics themselves—fit the criteria no less. They constitute or at least help to constitute "an objective form of that awareness."

In speaking of "our time" (after Auschwitz) in his major late statement, *Negative Dialectics* (1966), Adorno wrote: "The matters of true philosophical interest at this point in history are those in which Hegel, agreeing with tradition, expressed disinterest. They are non-conceptuality, individuality, and particularity—things which ever since Plato used to be dismissed as transitory and insignificant, and which Hegel labeled as 'lazy Existence'."[6] In other words, tradition was interested in conceptuality, ideas and generality (universals), and Platonism is concomitant with this tradition; but according to Adorno in the twentieth century, or coming to a head then, for good or evil, matters of true philosophical interest were turned on their head. Marx, Nietzsche, and Freud are mostly frequently cited as having much to do with this—and not, I think, unfairly.

When we reflect on our time, therefore, we do so in a manner different from Hegel and mainstream philosophy prior to him stretching back to Plato: for us, what is transitory and insignificant matters. I matter, for instance; so do you.[7] Often, for Adorno, and for us, this individuality and particularity is given non-conceptually in art, or, more precisely, *as* art. This is why we will be turning to artists—writers—in thinking through enchantment, rather than, as we might, to philosophers. We will turn to Proust, Rilke, Lou Salomé, and Goethe, more or less great writers, as they are regarded, but we might have made the same points we are going to make in this book in another book via some painters or musicians. But obviously the written word lends itself more easily to talking about writing than about music or painting if we cannot together sample the music or the painting. With any art, though, the point is that it does not represent: it incarnates or embodies and therefore it has a being of its own and, we might say, it gives being, because we who experience it may be fortified by it—even, as we shall see, to the point of death and beyond.

The approach to enchantment through the experience of art does not reduce to easy remedies that might come under the banner of "re-enchantment." The problem with re-enchantment, and why we will assiduously avoid its mention, is that it reduces too easily to ideology, to, in other words, a form of social coercion where enchantment is at the behest of the self-appointed "enchanters." Such ideology may have enchantment on its tongue, but it is totalitarian at its heart: wanting to impose enchantment "from above" or inculcate it "from below." It can never be proper enchantment. We shall not concern ourselves here with ideology like this. Practical freedom is the precondition of enchantment. Practical freedom includes artistic freedom. I cannot "re-enchant" you, my reader: I can only point you to reading, listening, and gazing and to the true meaning and ultimate value of these pursuits. Practical freedom consists in taking them up.

In the *Negative Dialectics*, Adorno calls enchantment, most appropriately, "metaphysical experience."[8] It sounds almost religious—but is it?

Adorno was a friend of Samuel Beckett, the famous Paris-based Irish poet and dramatist who wrote *Waiting for Godot* (during 1948 and 1949). They shared a common attitude, hardly religious, but the kind of "irreverent reverence" that probably is suitable in an age where religious pietism and sanctimony are no longer sustainable. Beckett was not religious, but he was not *not* religious. It depends what you mean by *religious*. If we mean by "religious" experience, or "metaphysical experience," to use Adorno's term, a science of experience which is true and in which our inner sensibility and sensitivity (our soul) corresponds with outer reality (the world as it appears to be), then we will speak of "religious" experience, although this is probably to redefine the term, perhaps radically so for some readers. However, this is an old idea in philosophy, going back to Kant at the end of the eighteenth century. We might ask on the basis of this definition: what kind of religion is it that would eschew a science of experience such as just described? Not one worthy of belief, I would think. But in this sense "true religion" is yet to come, for we do not yet have a correspondence between our inner life and the world around us, which will vary from place to place and over time in any case. We do not yet have this correspondence and perhaps we never will, and yet the activity which works for it is the activity of true religion and true art. Having said this, suggestively, not dogmatically; dialogically, not authoritatively, we are in deep water. But both Adorno and Beckett had precisely this sensibility that I have just described "after Kant."

I heard somewhere, for example, that Beckett was strolling along a Parisian boulevard one fine spring day with a friend, a visitor to the city, and the friend, looking up at the clear blue sky, took a long breath and said, "This is such a perfect day! It makes you feel glad to be alive!" Beckett responded: "I wouldn't go that far!" Irish humor. It was irreverent reverence, such as that which fills *Waiting for Godot*.

There is an exchange between the two characters Clov and Hamm in *Endgame* (1957), a play by Beckett which Adorno analyzed in a famous essay. These two characters live in dustbins after the world has ended and all life has been destroyed, at least as far as they can tell—not that they really go anywhere: both are invalids: Hamm cannot stand up, and Clov cannot sit down.

CLOV: Do you believe in the life to come?
HAMM: Mine was always that.
[Exit CLOV]

Adorno said, "He lets *a twisted secular metaphysics* shine through, with a Brechtian commentary."[9] I think this is the answer to our question above. Is "metaphysical experience," or enchantment, religious? At least, is it so in a time such as ours, in a culture such as ours, when religious dogmatism, pietism, and sanctimony are no longer sustainable? We will not pretend to be religious in our work of enchantment, but we will hold half-humorously to a Beckettian "twisted secular metaphysics" as good enough for us, for the time being.

A twisted secular metaphysics is as good a starting place as any in a time such as ours. Perhaps it is the only honest starting place. Certainly, to carry on with religious "business as usual" as if nothing "ultimate"—at least for us in western culture—has happened is either brainless or shallow. But "Auschwitz" is no neat marker either, as Levinas reminds us: "Since the end of the war, bloodshed has not ceased. Racism, imperialism, and exploitation remain ruthless. Nations and individuals expose one another to hatred and contempt, fearing destitution and destruction."[10] And therefore I would extend Adorno's fateful words on poetry and Auschwitz. Auschwitz (as the name which by convention in the survivor's literature stands for itself and for all the names of the death camps) shows among other things that rationality may well serve barbarism and the ends of pitiless mass murderers. This event—at least consciousness of it—terminates the dream of the Enlightenment project that would see reason lead us to a better world. Certainly we cannot do without reason. But reason does not (in and of itself) naturally incline to the good as had been expected. Reason needs criteria, as the greatest thinkers, Plato, Aristotle, Augustine, and Kant realized. But in extending Adorno I would point to the other side of the world, and the names of Hiroshima and Nagasaki. These names show the dream of technology as advancing humanity is no less catastrophic than the dream of reason. Certainly we are much better off with technology. But I want to note the huge difference between the two catastrophes, Auschwitz and Hiroshima. While the Jewish Holocaust, was rationalistic, planned, and bureaucratically organized, and the Nazis did name searches, going right back into the records, systematically digging for Jewish names, in order to identify them and flush them out, at Hiroshima the names of people were irrelevant and did not factor. The evil was done clinically, from a distance, in the blink of an eye. While the Jewish Holocaust required a North European work ethic, with all the implied industriousness, the Japanese Holocaust was "a technological achievement," as instant as flicking a light switch, as spectacular as a Hollywood disaster movie. Though only a few years separate Auschwitz from Hiroshima, they are epochally different from each other in their meaning for us today; although as Marguerite Duras has powerfully shown, the catastrophes can hardly be understood apart from each other.[11] Hiroshima belongs to the computer age, the age to come. Auschwitz came out of the past, out of the peculiarity of Christian hatred of Jews, out of the Middle Ages. Auschwitz belongs to the European age, Hiroshima to the American. And by "European" and "American" I do not mean those places or their peoples as such, but I mean *the spirit* of those places and peoples that also reaches right around the world and touches every place and almost every person.

All this must be backdrop for any talk of enchantment today. Again, Levinas: "At no other time has *historical experience weighed so heavily upon ideas*; or, at least, never before have the members of one generation been more aware of that weight."[12]

Levinas goes on to say that this brings with it a new more-or-less conscious sense of anxiety. Of course, anxiety is antithetical to enchantment. The more anxiety abroad and in our hearts and heads, the less the possibility of enchantment; conversely, the more enchantment in society and within us, the less there is to be needlessly anxious about. The work of enchantment in a time such as ours is a work against anxiety, which is such a governing mood, self-sustaining, and undermining. Also Levinas goes on to say that this anxiety brings with it an increased awareness of responsibility; this is not just the "global responsibility" we hear so much about today from those parading on the "world stage," but a personal responsibility which is down to each of us and not merely "up to the politicians" or those seemingly in power.

No doubt there are things we need to be anxious about, particularly where we fail in responsibility to one another. But to be dominated by anxiety about the end of the world, as many people are, is frankly absurd and self-indulgent. To have a "doomsday" mentality, as many people do, is to be dominated by an unhealthy imagination; it can only bring on those things, if they are even possible, rather than avert them.

Our milieu, in which we must consider enchantment, or the possibility of metaphysical experience, is certainly one that is post-modern, in the sense that the great certainties of modernity are gone, destroyed by our own hand. The great guiding myth of Progress, for example, is dubious. The great progress of the nineteenth century led to the disasters of the twentieth. The Great Leap Forward in China led to untold millions starving to death. The splitting of the atom enabled Hiroshima and Nagasaki, and so on. We know progress is as destructive as it is progressive, and so we are skeptical, but it is a healthy skepticism. We do not want "a brave new world" or a "great leap forward"—if we have any sense. And so, sometimes our anxiety is telling us something we need to take cognizance of. Our post-modernity has moved from a modernity governed by big ideology to an age of interpretation, which is, of its nature, a pluralistic age, as interpretation brings multiple perspectives to bear. This is a good thing though. It enjoins us to dialogue with one another and to proceed on that basis, rather than, as in "the good old days," to enforce a "solution" from on high.

It is in terms of this dialogical situation of an age of interpretation that we now approach the work of enchantment.

Notes

1. Emmanuel Levinas, *Proper Names*, trans. Michael B. Smith (Stanford, CA: Stanford University, 1996), 122.
2. Søren Kierkegaard, *Sickness unto Death*, trans. Alastair Hannay (London: Penguin, 1989), 62-3.
3. The original quote is in Theodor Adorno, *Prisms*, trans. Samuel and Shierry Weber (Cambridge MA: MIT Press, 1981), 34. The short sentence I have quoted is actually a misquote, in as much as it only approximates a phrase from a longer sentence which itself is not usually quoted in full. The complete sentence is: "The critique of culture is confronted with the last stage in the dialectic of culture and barbarism: to write a poem after Auschwitz is barbaric, and that corrodes also the knowledge which expresses why it has become impossible to write poetry today." Adorno came back to this topic on three different occasions: in the *Negative Dialektik*, in *Ohne Leitbild*, and in *Noten zur Literatur IV*. Page references are to the *Gesammelte Schriften*, where more details can be found: *Prismen*, vol. 10a, p. 30 (1955); *Negative Dialektik*, vol. 06, pp. 355-6; *Ohne Leitbild*, vol. 10a, pp. 452-3; *Noten zur Literatur IV*, vol. 11, p. 603. (My thanks to Dr. Frederik van Gelder, Institut fuer Sozialforschung, Frankfurt University for this note.)

4. Adorno, *Metaphysics: Concepts and Problems*, trans. Edmund Jephcott (Stanford, CA: Stanford University, 2001), 434. (Henceforth: *Metaphysics*)
5. Ibid., 435.
6. Adorno, *Negative Dialectics*, trans. E.B. Ashton (London: Routledge, 1990), 8.
7. Adorno's "negative dialectics"—even from the name we can see—turns Hegel not just upside down, like Marx claimed, but inside out as well.
8. Adorno, *Negative Dialectics*, 373.
9. Adorno, *Can One Live After Auschwitz? A Philosophical Reader*, ed. Rolf Tiedmann (Stanford, CA: Stanford University, 2003), 293. Brechtian, perhaps because both self-effacing and reconstructive. Or Brechtian, more possibly, because of the level of uncertainty carried by characters; a bit like Keats' "negative capability"—the capacity we ought to have, especially if we are religious, *to live with questions* and, indeed, *to live off* them. Any religion worth its salt, any metaphysics too, must do that, and Adorno surely means as much by "metaphysical experience."
10. Levinas, *Proper Names*, 119.
11. Marguerite Duras, *Hiroshima Mon Amour*, trans. Richard Seaver (New York: Grove Press, 1961).
12. Levinas, *Proper Names*, 4.

3

"A little patch of yellow wall"

In this and the next three chapters we will turn our attention to the novelist Marcel Proust. He will be our first icon *through which* we will be enabled to discern the lineaments of our subject, enchantment, and the work of enchantment, just as, long ago (or perhaps still today in some homes and churches), through the icons on the wall or the *iconostasis*, one could discern from what was pictured the lineaments of divine beings. The icon is the descendent of the hieroglyph, where something *significant* is signified by a sign, and the holiest writing, where something of *ultimate* significance for us to know about life and death is written.

Death is one of the factors that radically disrupt enchantment. But within an enchanted life death loses its sting.

Until now we have followed some thoughts of the philosopher Adorno, and it is indeed he too who leads us to Proust. Adorno says, "*A more decisive contribution to these matters [to do with metaphysical experience], I believe, is made by Marcel Proust, whose work, as a precipitate and an exploration of the possibility of experience, should be taken extremely seriously from a philosophical point of view.*"[1] And we shall take him extremely seriously for what he brings into view about enchantment. But we shall serve ourselves here in two ways, for to read Proust's major novel is to engage the work of enchantment, the work of reading something properly *worth reading*. It is a work that invites us into another world in which we nonetheless can see our own world, and indeed we can see ourselves; it is a work which dispels useless anxiety by enabling us to see through it, so as suddenly to see through a delusion that has been besetting our imagination, or, in other cases, so as to see the funny side of something. To read Proust is an initiation and so, in this chapter and the next, we will serve ourselves in the first instance, as I said, by treating Proust as an icon to something else, and in the second instance, by being introduced to Proust and his world, if it is new to us and we have not read him already.

Proust's major novel, believed by many to be the greatest novel ever written, is a multi-volume work entitled in French, *À la recherche du temps perdu* (*Remembrance of Things Past* or *In Search of Lost Time*). It was published serially in eight parts in Paris between 1913 and 1927. Proust lived between 1871 and 1922, and so the last parts of his great novel were published posthumously. On the surface the novels are about *fin de siècle* high society in Paris, gently lampooning it; but that is the surface of the narrative. For Adorno, as for us, reading Proust is an induction into metaphysical experience, or enchantment, in the strong sense that we want to give it.

Proust is buried at the beautiful Père Lachaise Cemetery in Paris alongside other family members. He was homosexual and never married, although he regretted rather than celebrated his homosexuality. He had mixed feelings over almost everything, except things such as really good coffee, and then he was extremely fussy. He was a man of "private means" which he devoted wholly to the work of literature. Information about him may easily be obtained and so I will not reiterate much here. Most famously, Proust lived as a recluse in his apartment at 102, Boulevard Haussmann, where he had the room where he spent most time, the bedroom, where he would write and sleep, writing at night, sleeping all day, lined in cork to block out noise and disturbance.[2]

The illustration of metaphysical experience or enchantment has to do with the death of the writer Bergotte in the volume entitled *The Captive* (1923). And here, at last, we will be entering into Proust's world, letting it enter our own, letting it captivate us; for to be captivated by the right things is to be enchanted. A child can be enchanted by almost anything, and even quite terrible things will not disenchant a little girl or boy; but gradually, with time, disenchantment will dawn on them, if it is not forced upon them first. So we are prone from the first for enchantment, we are geared for it, and by that I do not mean a childish "magical" sense of enchantment with fairies or scary monsters, but enchantment in the strong sense, which we will also call metaphysical experience; it comes through art as the quintessence of life and the objectification of it, as this or that art object.

Bergotte had gone, in the worst of health, on his "last legs" as we say, to gaze once again at a painting on display in Paris, Vermeer's *Street in Delft*, at an exhibition of Dutch paintings lent by the gallery at The Hague, "a picture which he adored and imagined that he knew by heart." But he had learnt from one of the art critics that "a little patch of yellow wall (which he could not remember) was so well painted that it was, if one looked at it by itself, like some priceless specimen of Chinese art, of a beauty that was sufficient in itself."[3] Not recalling the "little patch of yellow wall" and desiring to feast his eyes upon it, even if it was the last thing he did, he left the house and set out one fine morning for the art gallery. "At last he came to the Vermeer which he remembered as more striking, more different from anything else that he knew, but in which, thanks to the critic's article, he remarked for the first time some small figures in blue, that the ground was pink, and finally the precious substance of the tiny patch of yellow wall. His giddiness increased..." Bergotte, in a state of mortal dis-ease, reflects about his works, his great books, not without melancholy: "'My last books are too dry. I ought to have gone over them with several coats of paint, made my language exquisite in itself, like this little patch of yellow wall.' Meanwhile he was not unconscious of the gravity of his condition." As his life hangs in the balance, Bergotte imagines all his life on one side of the scale and the little patch of yellow wall on the other side, outweighing his life, but "so beautifully painted in yellow." Bergotte sinks down into death as he sits in the public gallery before the painting, muttering to himself, "Little patch of yellow wall, with a sloping roof, little patch of yellow wall." Perhaps now he, Bergotte, knows Vermeer's *Street in Delft* perfectly. Absolutely. To know one thing absolutely, to know it even more intimately than one's own creations, one's own offspring;

this is something great. It is an enchantment. It is metaphysical experience.

This is an exemplary death.

But there is a direct link between metaphysical experience and immortality, and resurrection—noting that immortality and resurrection are usually ideas at odds that do not fit together. Normally, immortality is seen as an idea where the body is dispensable as far as the immortal soul is concerned; and resurrection is a notion that indicates the unity of body and soul that dies or comes back to life together: body and soul cannot survive apart from each other. Yet, they do here. This link between Bergotte's death and metaphysical experience (basically Bergotte's legitimate enchantment with the art of Vermeer) is the reason why Adorno draws our attention to Proust's account—although, as we will go on to see, Proust's whole work has to do with metaphysical experience, and in a profound sense. Proust is not to be thought "un-philosophical" because, as we shall see directly, he combines immortality with resurrection, which metaphysicians and theologians religiously keep apart. In 1927 Heidegger published *Being and Time*, indeed an influential philosophical tome, but Proust, in the judgment of Adorno, had better things to say on the subject of being and time. And the greatest of modern philosophers, Hegel, is reversed by Proust, in that Hegel's idealism—his conceptuality and universalism—are totally lacking in Proust, whose focus is ever on the absolute uniqueness of the trivial and particular. And then, his unselfconscious philosophical prowess to one side, at the literary level, Proust exhibits as no writer had ever done before him at such uninterrupted length, and with such astonishing veracity, what one critic has called "versatility in depth." In other words, Proust is both a philosopher and a psychologist. To do philosophy or psychology without him is to make a big mistake.

But does he speak to a time such as ours? I raise this question because we have said in the last chapter that a time such as ours is described as "post-modern" because it is characterized by uncertainty about those things which drove modernity from the Enlightenment of the late eighteenth century to the wars of the twentieth. We are uncertain about modernity's strong sense of self, its belief in progress, and its idealism. Perhaps we are disillusioned with modernism, perhaps a lot of things are questionable to us; a later age will have to write our history and humankind will be wise in retrospect. However, we must attest that an artwork can speak diachronically, across time, to a time not its own. Proust's work is such a work. It spoke to the literary elites in his time; it speaks much more broadly, to almost any literate person of our culture, in our time. Some works are like this: over time they gain power to speak and they keep speaking into the times. The optimum example is those writings regarded by our culture as Scriptures. The Sermon on the Mount in Matthew's Gospel does not go out of date. It was written for a time but has a sense, in retrospect, of being written for all time: it stands therefore as a "testament," not merely of "what was," but of what should be; and it continues to be a revelation, serving to wake us up, to bring us to our senses, and so on. This is a strong example, but other writings have the same quality: they speak across the periods of history with a message that it is our peril to forget; the Greek tragedies, Shakespeare's plays, the Russian novel are such examples. And Proust belongs to this ilk. Yes, he wrote in another time from ours, but what he wrote bears on our time. Rilke and Goethe, the other two writers who are our icons by which we may discern enchantment, are like this too. Doubtless, time has many hidden rules, "time-bends," as Arthur Miller memorably called them.

From the point of view of *our* time, after so much disaster, with the kind of consciousness of disaster we have now and the sense of responsibility for ourselves and others that we have learned, we are well positioned to appreciate works that *stand the test of time*. This is ultimately the criterion for true art: work which stands the test of time; work which, after centuries, can and indeed *must enchant us*, if we are to flourish.

Bergotte had seen the little patch of yellow wall and died doing so: "He was dead. Permanently dead? Who shall say? Certainly our experiments in spiritualism prove no more than the dogmas of religion that the soul survives death. All that we can say is that everything is arranged in this life as though we entered it carrying the burden of obligation contracted in a former life; there is no reason inherent in the conditions of life on this earth that can make us consider ourselves obliged to do good, to be fastidious, to be polite even, nor to make a talented artist consider himself obliged to begin over again a score of times a piece of work the admiration aroused by which will matter little to his body devoured by worms like the patch of yellow wall painted with so much knowledge and skill by an artist who must for ever remain unknown and is barely identified under the name of Vermeer. All these obligations which have not their sanction in our present life seem to belong to a different world, founded upon kindness, scrupulosity, self-sacrifice, a world entirely different from this, which we leave in order to be born into this world, before perhaps returning to the other to live once again beneath the sway of those unknown laws which we have obeyed because we bore their precepts in our hearts, knowing not whose hand had traced them there—those laws to which every profound work of the intellect brings us nearer and which are invisible only—and still!—to fools. So that the idea that Bergotte was not wholly and permanently dead is by no means improbable.

They buried him, but all through the night of mourning, in the lighted windows, his books arranged three by three kept watch like angels with outspread wings and seemed, for him who was no more, the symbol of his resurrection."[4]

Of course, we cannot help thinking of Proust and his books lined on our shelves, three by three, and of the burden of obligation he carried into life and which is set forth in those volumes.

This painting by Vermeer really exists. What is so extraordinary, and so Proustian, as once again his art outsmarts life, is that critics are divided on exactly where this little patch of yellow wall actually is in the painting. There are three main theories, each pointing to a different patch of yellow wall. So Proust defies the objectivists, even in death. Perhaps (this is my surmise) those art critics do not know the painting in the depth Bergotte knew it, and they would not recognize that little patch of yellow wall until they do; then they will find it, not before. But there is a catch. To know that painting as Bergotte knew it, one must be prepared to suffer unto death, as he did.

Enchantment is that little patch of yellow wall. By reading, listening, or gazing, we must find that little patch of yellow wall for ourselves, by which of course I mean, what it is for us. Short of a tragedy or a ruinous childhood, we die of what we live for; and the enchanted life is one that can live for a painting, such as that by Vermeer, and know it by heart, so that, despite all consequences, even the most ultimate, we are moved, literally moved, if we hear something about it that we cannot remember and do not think we ever knew. That is to be moved by the wisdom of love, philosophy herself. For philosophy in this case is feminine, and she leads us on. She is feminine because she speaks to our soul; and only in our soul, thanks to our senses, do we hear her.

Notes

1. Adorno, *Metaphysics*, 463. (Italics added to original) Adorno brushes aside misgivings about "literature" and "philosophy," naming poor Herr Bollnow, now forgotten, and adding that if he is qualified to contribute seriously to discussion on metaphysics, why should Marcel Proust not be? Of course, for Herr Bollnow, we can fill in names better known to us and ask the same question. But today, thankfully, in the mainstream at least, these justifications are hardly necessary.
2. The best work about him in my view remains that by André Maurois, *À la recherche de Marcel Proust* (1949), translated into English by Gerard Hopkins as *The Quest for Proust* (London: Penguin Books, 1962).
3. Proust, *The Captive*, Part One, trans. C.K. Scott-Montcrieff (London: Chatto & Windus, 1951), 249ff.
4. Ibid., 251.

4

"Nothing more than a few words"

The enchantment of a few words, simply spoken, and the "metaphysical experience" of this is what we come to in this chapter. What we want to show is beautifully illustrated by a passage in Part Two of the first volume of *Remembrance of Things Past*, which is entitled *Swann's Way* (1913); it concerns Monsieur Swann and his lover, Odette de Crécy.

Swann mixes in the very best circles of high society. He is financially secure and belongs, as his English lineage suggests, to the new order of wealthy business interests, rather than to the old order of pure aristocratic blood. However, the English rather than American background suggests aristocracy, and the business interests merely indicate new money rather than anything which might be suggestive of the crass, commercial or exploitative. Swann is refined, he has taste, he is an art lover; in fact, he is writing an article that he has been researching on the painter Vermeer. He has something in common then with Bergotte.

Swann has become infatuated with Odette. She is single, seemingly a woman of her own means—which Swann takes for granted at first—and, compared to him, somewhat more bohemian; at least, that would seem to be part of the attraction. One day, he goes to tea with her. She tells him about her devotion to Our Lady of Laghetto, who, once, when she was living in Nice, cured her of a deadly illness, and whose medal she always carries on her person, convinced of its curative power. She makes the tea just right and she says, "You see, I know just how you like it." And he thinks, as he leaves, "What fun it would be to have a little woman like that in a place where one could always be certain of finding, what one never can be certain of finding, a really good cup of tea."[1]

On his second visit, he takes her an engraving which had come up in conversation and which she had asked to see. He falls in love. But this sounds bland. Look how enchantment leads to love and blends with it:

> As she stood there, beside him, brushing his cheek with the loosened tress of her hair, bending one knee in what was almost a dancer's pose, so that she could lean without tiring herself over the picture, at which she was gazing, with a bended head, out of those great eyes, which seemed so weary and so sullen when there was nothing to animate her, Swann was struck by her resemblance to the figure of Zipporah, Jethro's Daughter, which is to be seen in one of the Sistine frescoes.[2]

Enchantment, or metaphysical experience, is "aesthetic" in requiring a gaze which can transfigure and transmute what seems to be the case into what is, given by true art. Such art is true because it declares beauty. Pictorial and plastic art as living beauty is always beheld in a moment in the midst of a gaze—the object is merely "such as it is," material for transfiguration. Love and being in love is the instance most well known to all of us of what I am talking about. Loving someone makes a huge difference in how you see them. You see a haggard white-haired old woman on her last legs who really means nothing to you; I see my grandmother. Falling in love, we fall into enchantment. The one we love causes us to see the whole world differently and even to *be* in the world differently. Young singles are not just looking for a "life-partner" but for the one who will effect the change and make them, in their being, different. This is metaphysical experience.

Religion of course picks up on it and uses it. For instance, in the case of Peter, James, and John, the disciples of Jesus who follow him up the mountain and suddenly see him a figure of light, talking with Moses and Elijah. They see Jesus as he really is and, if they had been wrong, if he had not been transfigured and had not indeed been talking with Moses and Elijah, Christianity should not exist, for there would be merely a man to base it on, a good man possibly, but not *that* man.

And so, Swann sees Odette, all of a sudden, in a new light. But what is interesting about this passage, which speaks volumes about Swann, is that he is prone to transmute reality into art as part of his ordinary perception.

> He had always found a peculiar fascination in tracing in the paintings of the Old Masters, not merely the general characteristics of the people whom he encountered in his daily life, but rather what seems least susceptible of generalization, the individual features of men and women whom he knew, as, for instance, in a bust of the Doge Lorendan by Antonio Rizzo, the prominent cheekbones, the slanting eyebrows, in short, a speaking likeness to his own coachman, Rémy; in the coloring of a Ghirlandaio, the nose of M. de Palancy; in the portrait by Tintoretto, the invasion of the plumpness of the cheek by an outcrop of whisker, the broken nose, the penetrating stare, the swollen eyelids of Dr. du Boulbon.[3]

From gazing, Swann has got "an eye" for things. He can see them more truly—for what they are. Things are trans-substantiated for him.

This metaphysical experience is a far cry from representation. Zipporah does not "represent" Odette at all for him: Zipporah *is* Odette. The theory of representation only obtains in lieu of metaphysical experience, where one really has no eye for things at all; and where one has a tendency to abstract and objectify, so that one thing stands outside another and may "represent" it. But "transubstantiation" and "transfiguration" are words that bespeak metaphysical experience. Enchantment has to do with recouping this experience, which should be part of our world, but often is not. In culture, philosophically speaking, enchantment has to do with reinstating aesthetics at the heart of metaphysics. What then has become of aesthetics?—one may justifiably ask. It has been turned into "theory of beauty" and "art theory," a mere branch of metaphysics. Whereas we are saying it is trunk and branch.

Something has happened in philosophy and in culture to extirpate aesthetics and castrate it and cast it out on a limb.

True aesthetic thinking today is not some limp appendage to a philosophy major; it is basic to philosophy, and it has to do with turning back this tide. Social critical theory, in the best instances of it, as in Adorno (a towering figure in this regard), can be good at the diagnosis of *why* this cultural slide toward disenchantment is the case. Obviously, roughly put, the total commercialization of culture ("the culture industries") has much to do with it; and this has to do with capitalism and the philosophy of cupidity by which capitalism justifies itself, alongside, of course, the myth of progress and the hubris of the new, all of which protest such criticisms with such avid self-serving justification.

Enchantment is a rallying cry in this context, because it stands outside capitalism. It is what capitalism can never produce and no money can buy. The word "enchantment" has been weakened and, of course, Disneyfied, in an attempt to ape it; but aping enchantment is as near as the capitalist interests will get to the real thing. The meaning, purpose, and truth of the humanities—that range of disciplines that once held surety for the life of a university at the educational heart of a culture and society—stand with "enchantment," with this word.

We need to understand the power of words for metaphysical experience though.

Swann, having fallen in love with Odette, now that he can relate her face to that of Jethro's Daughter, becomes infatuated with her. But she, it is evident, while inviting, while loving, is not always easy to pin down. Swann does not know where she is, and who she is with, as much as he would like. She always has an excuse for her unavailability which seems perfectly natural; but Swann is jealous of this "other" life invisible to him, from which he is excluded, which Odette leads.

One day, out of the blue, he receives an anonymous letter informing him of what surely must therefore be widely known, except by him, that Odette is involved in various sexual liaisons, some of them lesbian. He is so thunderstruck that someone would write him such a disgraceful letter anonymously that, to begin with, he refuses to believe it; but gradually the words of the letter feed his latent jealousy. Now what we want to learn has to do with the metaphysical experience of the sound of words, that is, the utter captivating power words have to keep us in *their* being. Another way of saying it is to say that words carry soul; words can be soul-making, but they can also be soul-destroying. In fact, words are rarely ever neutral. Although this is of signal importance, we scarcely give it any credence—linguistics takes very little notice of it. Freud, the great soul-man, more than anyone, pays credence to what we are talking about.[4] And what we are talking about here is best understood in *literature*, especially in the works of the nineteenth-century novel, rather than those of the twentieth: in Balzac or the Brontës more than in James Joyce or Georges Perec, who we may, perhaps, admire for other reasons.

To make the point, I need to set the scene a little.

He went to see Odette. He sat down, keeping his distance from her. He did not dare embrace her, not knowing whether in her, or in himself, it would be affection or anger that a kiss would provoke. He sat there silent, watching their love expire.[5]

Then Proust begins to probe the experience of watching their love expire. His first dissection runs as follows:

"Odette, my darling," he began, "I know, I am being simply odious, but I must ask you a few questions. You remember what I once thought about you and Mme. Verdurin? Tell me, was it true? Have you, with her or anyone else, ever?"

She shook her head, pursing her lips together; a sign which people commonly employ to signify that they are not going, because it would bore them to go, when someone has asked, "Are you coming to watch the procession go by?" or "Will you be at the review?" But this shake of the head, which is thus commonly used to decline participation in an event that has yet to come, imparts for that reason an element of uncertainty to the denial of participation in an event that is past. Furthermore, it suggests reasons of personal convenience, rather than any definite repudiation, any moral impossibility. When he saw Odette thus make him a sign that the insinuation was false, he realized that it was quite probably true.

Proust had the knack, the gift, and the genius, of expressing exactly what we know we have almost thought, but somehow know we had not the words to actually think it; and then we see it in Proust, clearly written down, not only expressing perfectly the shadows of our presentiments, but actually extending them into domains we realize, somehow, we were unconscious of. We know the denial that seems rather to assent. We have witnessed ourselves Odette's body language and we have also read it the way Swann reads it. We can see Odette exactly.

Swann continues to be "odious" and to press her about his suspicions. He riles her, or she affects being riled. She blazes forth:

"Have you nearly done? What is the matter with you today? You seem to have made up your mind that I am to be forced to hate you, to curse you! Look, I was anxious to be friends with you again, for us to have a nice time together, like the old days; and this is all the thanks I get!"

However, he would not let her go, but sat there like a surgeon who waits for a spasm to subside that has interrupted his operation but need not make him abandon it.

Ironically, this superbly apt metaphor reinforces the image it makes by the brevity of its clinical incisiveness.

He suggests to her that he knows more than she thinks he knows and presses her to swear on her Laghetto medal: "'Tell me, upon your medal,'" he cajoles her, "'yes or no, whether you have ever done those things.'" Odette is cornered. All her ploys are to no avail:

"How on earth can I tell?" she was furious. "Perhaps I have, ever so long ago, when I didn't know what I was doing, perhaps two or three times."

The scene is set. We come to the point, about the power of words:

> Swann had prepared himself for all possibilities. Reality must, therefore, be something which bears no relation to possibilities, any more than the stab of a knife in one's body bears to the gradual movement of the clouds overhead, since, those words, "two or three times," carved as it were, a cross upon the living tissue of his heart. A strange thing, indeed, that those words, "two or three times," nothing more than a few words, words uttered in the air, at a distance, could so lacerate a man's heart, as if they had actually pierced it, could sicken a man, like a poison he had drunk.

Nothing more than a few words…And yet, who does not know what Proust is talking about? It is the power of words in and upon the soul that can take us up and bring us down, that can seal or break marriages, that are more powerful than kingdoms and empires, which, anyway, in the end, rely on nothing more than a few words…

The thoughts rush through Swann's mind as a horrifying dawning:

> The agony that he now suffered in no way resembled what he had supposed. Not only because, in the hours when he most entirely mistrusted her, he rarely imagined such a culmination of evil, but because, even when he did imagine that offence, it remained vague, uncertain, was not clothed in the particular horror which had escaped with the words "perhaps two or three times," was not armed with that specific cruelty, as different from anything that he had known as a new malady by which one is attacked for the first time.

Proust's analysis unpicks Swann's soul; it is psychoanalysis in the proper sense. What we realize though, at the level of metaphysical experience, is that words move us. Normally we imagine we "use" language and that it is "at our command"; but this is true much more minimally than we realize and in fact this dogma with respect to words (actually it is "the pragmatic attitude") prevents us from seeing the truth. Language is not a "tool" of some kind for "doing a job." But this is the illusion we labor under with language in general, and words in particular, in our "communication" culture, which is actually not really a culture at all, but the dominance of an industry filling in where culture once was and simulating some aspects of it, perhaps for our reassurance that it is all for the better. In fact, words move us. Swann's "laceration" by the words which are as vague and ordinary as to be almost meaningless, "two or three times," is metaphysical experience; it is the *enchantment of words*. Suddenly, part of what he discovers in this interview with Odette, as Proust explicitly says, is "a strange thing." The strange thing is the encounter with words in their reality as able to carve a cross on the living tissue of his heart. Words had always had this potential. Words were moving him all along, from the time Odette had said, pouring his tea, "You see, I know just how you like it." Perhaps these same words she had uttered under quite different circumstances, even maybe to Mme. Verdurin.

Our power over words is much less than their power over us. Our power is mainly negative: the power to empty words. This is the power of modern barbarism with its communication industry, which makes believe it is a brighter better world, when it is actually only so in some minimal respects, or only so in some areas, such as medicine; quite possibly we are losing much more than we are gaining. Perhaps we now *lack* the necessary vocabulary to recoup our losses. Words will not come to our rescue. Indeed, words have withdrawn from us, and left us with all sorts of brand names instead of proper names, and initialisms standing for every conceivable thing. We feel proud of the way we "initialize" our company, or of whatever it is "for short"; but in fact it is a shame. A shame we do not feel any more.

Words and feelings, words and soul, go together. Psychoanalysis is the talking cure. At least the Freudian inception of psychoanalysis understood the power of words to move us and to transform, transfigure, and transubstantiate us, even if, later, the field of research called psychoanalysis and the craft of carrying it out were destroyed by technical pragmatists who then, in control of the whole thing, professionalized it in their own image.

Letting words shed their power into our inner sensitivity and sensibility is the way to read proper poetry. Proper poetry is not simply versifying, nor is it just self-expressing. A true poet makes himself or herself sensitive to language to a morbid degree of sensitivity so that the poet, from this depth of immersion in words, can say something to move us, so that we too know the power of the word. Not that it is the poet's intention necessarily to move us. According to Lou Salomé, Rilke's poetry "is all a release into himself not a form of communication."[6] "Poetry is his means of self-transfiguration."[7] The poet is an initiator of metaphysical experience. He or she initiates us, the readers, into metaphysical experience. That is to say, they captivate our imagination; they enchant us. It is the sheer condensation of the poetic word that makes it so powerful and unlike other utterances.

Proust's account of the interview between Swann and Odette is wonderful, both at the level of comic entertainment, and also at the profound level of metaphysical experience.

As the passage continues, Swann tries to draw Odette out as to times and places: "'I only wished to know whether it (these liaisons) had been since I knew you. It's only natural. Did it happen here, ever? You can't give me any particular evening, so that I can remind myself what I was doing at the time?'"

Caught off guard by his endearing tone of entreaty, and having already made her confession, so feeling already absolved, Odette paints for Swann a little picture of one such incident in the Bois. She reminds Swann they had been dining with the Princesse des Laumes and a woman at the next table to where they were sitting had made a pass at Odette: "'At first I just yawned,' Odette tells Swann, and said, 'No, I'm too tired, and I'm quite happy where I am, thank you.'" And she continues her story, with the woman's persistence. But suddenly, catching sight of the look on Swann's face, she clams up instantly and vehemently tells him off for making her tell him lies. The next paragraph starts ominously like this:

> This second blow struck at Swann was even more excruciating than the first...

Proust then gives in what follows a devastating prognostication of Swann's soul after listening to this little story, reconstructing it from her words and seeing it as clearly as if it were happening now, in his mind's eye.

And so the account goes on. At one level, it is the torment of Swann's love and jealousy that fire each other up, but at the level of metaphysical experience, the words, "two or three times" and "I knew what she was after" gain ascendancy and power over Swann that would have been unimaginable before, and these words replace other words, redolent of other scenes and memories.

The power of words to move us in manifold ways is at the core of *Remembrance of Things Past*. Usually, the words Proust shows moving his characters are, as we have seen in the case of Swann, of the most ordinary variety. The most famous example is the maid Françoise's words, "Mademoiselle Albertine has gone!" Marcel, in the story, had concluded, upon long reflection and memory, that he no longer loved her and it would be a relief to him to have her out of his life. "But now these words, 'Mademoiselle Albertine has gone!' had expressed themselves in my heart in the form of an anguish so keen that I would not be able to endure it for any length of time. And so what I had supposed to mean nothing to me was the only thing in my whole life."[8] Over the next 80 pages Proust depicts the dawning realization within Marcel of his true love for Albertine. And then news is brought to him of Albertine's death, "thrown against a tree when she was out riding."[9] Of course, the words that inform us of the death of one close to us are always going to have an absolute life-changing impact. Marcel is only beginning to digest this news when two letters from Albertine arrive in the post, letters written on two consecutive days before the accident happened. "For the death of Albertine to be able to suppress my suffering, the shock of the fall would have had to kill her not only in Touraine but in myself. There, never had she been more alive."[10]

The name Albertine is not just attached to the woman of that name, but is *in* Marcel, psychologically, and moreover it is actually *constitutive* of his inner sensibility and sensitivity. In *The Cities of the Plain* (*Sodome et Gomorrhe*, 1922), Albertine is about to get off the train at her stop. As she stands up and the train slows down, she finalizes what they have been talking about by sharing with Marcel the confidence that she is intimate, in the strongest sense of the word ("I always call them my two big sisters"), and has been so over a long period of time, with Mademoiselle Vinteuil and her "friend."

Marcel is stirred as he remembers the time, recorded for us back in Volume 1 of the novel, when he observed these two young women by chance and discovered that they were both sadistic lesbians.[11] Albertine moves to alight from the train at the same moment as Marcel's heart is torn unendurably by his association of her with these bad women, "just as if, notwithstanding the position independent of my body which Albertine's body seemed to be occupying a yard away from it, this separation in space, which an accurate draughtsman would have been obliged to indicate between us, was only apparent, and anyone who wished to make a fresh drawing of things as they really were would now have had to place Albertine, not at a certain distance from me, but inside me."[12]

Albertine is as much alive in him as she is in herself—not as two lives, but by extension. And this is how it is with us human beings. This is why we are embodied *souls*. This is why we are not individuals in the sense of "discrete entities"; psychosomatically, we are each part of each other. We never just exist *in* ourselves, even if we are totally selfish and live *for* ourselves alone. The name of Albertine and the real presence that the name bears will resound within Marcel as long as he lives; it may even kill him.

While bodily we are separate, as we can see, mere sight is deceptive, for my loved ones are "not at a certain distance from me, but inside me." Only when, instead of merely seeing, we *gaze* into their eyes do we see each other's reflection; this is not just an illusion: it is the truth: *there we really are.*

> As our vision is a deceiving sense, a human body, even when it is loved as Albertine's was, seems to us to be at a few yards', at a few inches' distance from us. And similarly with the soul that inhabits it. But *something* need only effect a violent change in the relative position of that soul to ourself, to shew us that she is in love with others and not with us, then by the beating of our dislocated heart we feel that it is not a yard away from us but within us that the beloved creature was. Within us, in regions more or less superficial. But the words, "That friend is Mlle. Vinteuil" had been the *Open, sesame* which I should have been incapable of discovering in myself, which had made Albertine penetrate to

the depths of my shattered heart. And the door that had closed behind her, I might seek for a hundred years without learning how it might be opened.[13]

Enchantment is essentially to do with the power of words. This is why poetry is absolutely central to it, and, to anything worthy of the name "culture." By poetry of course I mean the real thing, not self-expressivism, which is what poetry is largely reduced to in our time. But if enchantment is essentially to do with the power of words, of course reading, listening, and gazing will be activities of the utmost importance. With reading and listening, the connection is obvious. With gazing, if we recall Bergotte again, we will remember that it was his reading about the little patch of yellow wall which sent him on his quest. Gazing is never distinct from the power of words. These three words, "reading," "listening," and "gazing," themselves need to have ascendancy and power over our souls if we are to discover enchantment, if we are to be capable of it, if we are to be soul-making, not soul-destroying.

Notes

1. Proust, *Swann's Way*, Part Two, 5. (In the New York edition published by Albert & Charles Boni [1930], Parts One and Two are published together, 286ff.)
2. Ibid., 5–6.
3. Ibid., 6.
4. For instance, Freud, *The Psychopathology of Everyday Life*, trans. Anthea Bell (London: Penguin, 2002. In this work Freud shows words lodge within us and get stuck and cannot come out, with all kinds of psychologically symptomatic results.
5. Proust, *Swann's Way*, Part Two, trans. C. K. Moncrieff (London: Chatto & Windus, 1966), 200ff; New York one-volume edition, 468ff.
6. Lou Salomé, *The Freud Journal*, trans. Stanley A. Leavy (New York: Basic Books, 1964), 180.
7. Ibid., 182.
8. Proust, *The Sweet Cheat Gone*, Part One (*Albertine disparue*, 1925), trans. C. K. Moncrieff (London: Chatto & Windus, 1969), 1.
9. Ibid., 82.
10. Ibid., 85.
11. Proust, "The Way by Swann's," in *In Search of Lost Time*, I (1913), trans. Lydia Davis (London: Penguin, 2003), 160ff.
12. Proust, *Cities of the Plain*, Part Two, trans. C. K. Moncrieff (London: Chatto & Windus, 1968), 364.
13. Ibid., 379–80.

5

Vinteuil's Sonata

Before Swann's passion for Odette, at a time when he was still trying to "run into her" by chance, as lovers like to do, he would frequent Mme. Verdurin's salon. It was well below the circles he was used to, but Swann had the manners that allowed him to fit in to society at various levels; in other words, he had the common sense to distinguish the levels but to take none of them too seriously. At Mme. Verdurin's salon, he was fairly sure to run into Odette.

Again, this is the entertaining and comical surface of Proust, but there is another level, beneath this, that we are reading—for this is what proper reading entails.

The year before, at an evening party, he had heard a piece of music played on the piano and violin. At first he had appreciated only the material quality of the sounds which those instruments secreted.

This is the level of "hearing" something.

At first Swann had only *heard* the music. "And it had been a source of keen pleasure when, below the narrow ribbon of the violin-part, delicate, unyielding, substantial, and governing the whole, he had suddenly perceived, where it was trying to surge upwards in a flowing tide of sound, the mass of the piano-part, multi-form, coherent, level, and breaking everywhere in melody like the deep tumult of the sea, silvered and charmed into a minor key by the moonlight. But at a given moment, without being able to distinguish any clear outline, or to give a name to what was pleasing him, suddenly enraptured, he had tried to collect, to treasure in his memory the phrase or harmony—he knew not which—that had just been played, and had opened and expanded his soul just as the fragrance of certain roses, wafted upon the moist air of evening, has the power of dilating our nostrils."[1]

Beyond merely "hearing" when we really listen, which can only happen where there is something to be listened to, and heard in depth, at another level we are involved with metaphysical experience. In this case, it is enchanting. We said earlier that not all metaphysical experience is enchanting. The creative experience of producing the artworks or literature of enchantment is not in itself enchanting: it is suffering—as the biography of nearly any artist can tell us. But the recipient, on the other hand, is graced, as Swann is when he hears this music. He has no sense from it of the personal difficulties the composer has, as a single parent, raising his daughter, for instance.

Having listened, and heard anew, heard what he had not and could not hear before, Swann's soul, Proust says, "opened and expanded" like nostrils that dilate when they catch a beautiful scent.

We know enchantment when this happens to us. Music is actually the foremost way into such experience.

"Proust," Adorno said, "should be read with the idea of those great cathedrals in mind, dwelling on the concrete without grasping prematurely at something that yields itself not directly but only through its thousand facets."[2]

> Proust's spirit was completely metaphysical in the midst of a world that forbids the language of metaphysics: this tension is the moving spirit behind his whole work.[3]

Proust is a lesson to philosophers after Auschwitz. "In Proust...the relationship of the whole to the detail is not that of an overall architectonic plan to the specifics that fill it in: it is against precisely that, against the brutal untruth of a subsuming form forced on from above, that Proust revolted. Just as the temperament of his work challenges customary notions about the general and the particular and gives aesthetic force to the dictum from Hegel's *Logic* that the particular is the general and vice versa, with each mediated through the other, so the whole, resistant to abstract outlines, crystallizes out of the intertwined individual presentations."[4]

It is in music that this scintillation between the universal and particular takes the bodiless yet bodily form of notes which may actually be sounded and heard.

Proust has played a central role in my intellectual economy for decades, and I simply could not imagine him absent from the continuity of my concerns.[5]

The "little phrase" that Swann heard and that dilated his soul stuck in his memory and kept coming back to him. It haunted him. This is what it is to be enchanted.

"And this indefinite perception," Proust writes, this haunting, "would continue to smother in its molten liquidity the motifs which now and then emerge, barely discernible, to plunge again and disappear and drown; recognized only by the particular kind of pleasure which they instill, impossible to describe, to recollect, to name; ineffable."[6] This is part of a full-page anatomical dissection, by Proust, of listening.

Reading, listening, and gazing, in the enchanted sense, where "enchanted" is a basic word which names a mode of existing and, more importantly, a soulful being, is ineffable experience.

Normally we do not think of reading as ineffable but as a plain fact. We can, so we believe, see someone doing it. As for "gazing," this is merely for the idle. Listening is important when instructions are being given. These are the pragmatic *perversions* of what are more actually ineffable acts of soul.

But this appreciation of ineffability is precisely what we have lost today. Pragmatism, the philosophy of the New World, can never provide it. Pragmatism is a form of philosophical blindness toward pages for which there is no Braille; it is a form of deafness which can "hear" but not listen; and as for gazing...let us not waste our time!

Proust does not just write of another world in terms of *fin de siècle* Paris, but, more importantly, he writes of an even more distant world, of metaphysical experience, of enchantment.

We cannot turn the clock back to Paris, then; but metaphysical experience is a moral obligation for us now, today, and tomorrow, if we are human, not neo-barbarians. Technology—for all its uses and purposes, many of which are entertaining and fun, others of more serious use-value—can never produce or reproduce enchantment. Technology is good to serve culture; but capitalist forces are replacing culture with technology and redefining culture in terms of the *technē*. I realize the phrase "capitalist forces" is weak and abstract. Normally it means some faceless "economic" forces, but the human reality behind the phrase is more basic. The emotional forces of greed, faith, and fear underlie and spur on the "economic forces" or "forces of capitalism" just as they oil the wheels of fortune—for the global stock market is really nothing but gambling. And this gambling has become a law unto itself.

To read Proust is to know this, because we are transported from our world of monstrous vanities and illusions to his, where, for all its faults—and in its innocence, compared to our world today—enchantment was in the air.

Poor Swann, having heard "the little phrase" and remembered it, then keeps *almost* hearing it, thinking he is hearing it or about to hear it, only to be disappointed. They were other phrases, facsimiles, and fugitive versions of his little phrase. Just as he was about, once more, to experience "the little phrase" as he had at first, it would die away, as the music moved contrary to the memory that was so real.

This is still to be enchanted. Swann had tried to find out from his musical friends what this little phrase was, where it had come from, but to no avail. "Vividly though he could recall the exquisite and inexpressible pleasure which the little phrase had given him, and he could see, still, before his eyes the forms it traced in outline, he was quite incapable of humming over to them the air."[7] Eventually, unable to fix it with a proper name, and therefore to find it and hear it again, he forgot it, or, more precisely, it left him, it let him be.

One evening, at Mme. Verdurin's, as usual, someone was engaged to play the piano, and then, "suddenly, after a high note held on through two whole bars, Swann saw it approaching, stealing forth from underneath that resonance, which was prolonged and stretched out over it, like a curtain of sound, to veil the mystery of its birth—and recognized, secret, whispering, articulate, the airy and fragrant phrase that he had loved. And it was so peculiarly itself, it had so personal a charm, which nothing else could have replaced, that Swann felt as though he had met, in a friend's drawing room, a woman whom he had seen and admired once, in the street, and had despaired of ever seeing her again. Finally the phrase withdrew and vanished, pointing, directing, diligent among the wandering currents of its fragrance, leaving upon Swann's features a reflection of its smile."

Now, Swann could capture the ineffable. How do you do that? He got up, crossed the room and, thanking the pianist, Vinteuil, profusely, found out from Mme. Verdurin the piece was known as "Vinteuil's sonata." So there he had it. He had the proper name by which this ineffable object could be pinned down. Now, not only could he listen to it when he liked, now that he knew its name, but he could read about it too. "Then he asked for some information about this Vinteuil; what else he had done, and at what period of his life he had composed the sonata—what meaning the little phrase could have had for him, that was what Swann wanted most to know."

Once one is able to be enchanted, which has to do with being inwardly open—although, as we shall say, not just this: it has to do with education in the humanities—then it becomes a way of life. The knowledge Swann may gain about the sonata, the very intimately personal nature of this knowledge, will lead him forward to new enchantment, and the knowledge that he gains of himself will become, as he looks back, his development.

Notes

1. Proust, *Swann's Way*, Part One, 287; New York one-volume edition, 268.
2. Adorno, *Notes to Literature*, Volume One, trans. Rolf Tiedman (New York: Columbia, 1991), 175.
3. Ibid., 183.
4. Ibid., 174.
5. Adorno, *Notes to Literature*, Volume Two, trans. Rolf Tiedman (New York: Columbia, 1992), 312. (Italics added to original)
6. Proust, *Swann's Way*, Part One, 288; New York one-volume edition, 268.
7. Proust, *Swann's Way*, Part One, 291f; New York one-volume edition, 272f.

6

The Proper Name

This is our last chapter for which Proust is treated iconically as that *through which* we discern the lineaments of what enchantment might mean in a time such as ours and, therefore, what the work of enchantment—reading, listening, and gazing—might entail.

Let us just take stock for a moment and list what we have learned. Broadly, enchantment means to be captivated by a world not our own, one which is more beautiful than our own and which, indeed, captures our devotion. Such a world as this, Proust inhabited. He was captivated by his own world, humble though it really was; its grandiosity was just an illusion. And is not this always our reality? Humble in fact; any grandiosity, an illusion. Broadly again, enchantment is an attunement of our existence, one we must make if we are to live and die aright, that is, *well*.

Referring back to Bergotte, enchantment means a life in which devotion to *art* is pre-eminent. This is devotion to an art which has stood the test of time (Vermeer, in this case) rather than the trivia of the day, which will be forgotten tomorrow, and rightly so. Such art is art which one will stagger out to see on pain of death. Proust himself wrote like this, writing upon pain of death, writing himself in fact to death; but what more enchanted a way to live? No wonder he has so much to teach us.

And then, referring back to our account of the way *words* affect us. Sometimes, as in the case of Swann, enchantment itself can be delusory, for we can become enchanted in a way that leads to suffering and in fact causes us suffering; but in that case, even our suffering is blessed—that is, covered—by enchantment. We are enchanted sufferers. Suffering does not necessarily dispel enchantment; enchantment may overarch it. Sometimes we will be enchanted by the wrong things, by the wrong people. This is where "the moral compass" comes in to guide us. Swann's saving grace is that in all his great delusion about Odette, he is charming and so is she. What is charming is as related to art as it is to religion, which is why Swann could equate his lover with a painting on the wall in the Vatican, Christendom's holiest shrine. What we learn is that enchantment is bounded by what is charming and what is lovable here, and it is guided too by that. Only if we get completely lost will we require our moral compass, and so it is important to know where it is, at least, and not to lose it.

Finally, referring back to Vinteuil's "little phrase," it is *music* that speaks to the soul most directly, and, as Adorno thought too, it is the most "metaphysical" of the arts and, in that sense, the closest one to philosophy herself. Music, like the other arts, educates—in the sense of *educes*, which means *brings out*—our inner sensibility and sensitivity. In plain English, music is good for the soul, it steadies and nourishes the soul, and it opens the soul to the possibility of being enchanted. In other words, music tunes our emotions by eliciting the true feeling consonant with a note, chord, passage, etc. Good music does this, but bad music has the reverse effect: it deadens the soul and kills our inner sensibility and sensitivity. It is the soul that is the measure of good or bad music and, more precisely, the truth of emotions as *value judgments*. An emotion is also a judgment about something, not merely, as we are liable to believe, a "reaction." Of course, accompanying these emotions are thoughts and ideas, and good music will create a harmony between them. This is not to say that harmonious music is necessarily good music, for music exists in time and is a child of time, and, in different times, people will have different ears for different things—for jazz, for instance. Art (classical) music itself recognizes these changes in time, as we see from its long history. Music can sensitize us in every conceivable way. But it is a primary source for enchantment and, of course, listening to music is the work of enchantment; this is the music, like Vinteuil's little phrase, which really enters our soul and our life.[1]

Names have a music of their own, and to this notion we now turn. Certain names can vouch for enchantment. Proust devotes two sections of *Remembrance of Things Past* to names.

We have noted the significance of the name Auschwitz as a touchstone of reality.

Names are not only touchstones of reality but also they are touchstones of enchantment and metaphysical experience. The first book of *Remembrance of Things Past* is entitled *Combray*. A place-name. And the importance of names flows right through the whole work. The name is what connects the past to the present and to survival into the future. The name is caught up with being and time. The name also comes out from within, from our inner sensitivity and sensibility, the soul, to the outer world, where it becomes "common." The name is a crossway, therefore, of the dynamic: from within to without, from past to future.

This is why names are important, and "proper" to reality. Even big capitalist corporations (and small ones too) see the point of this, even if not philosophically; hence brand names. Names resonate with our inner sensitivity and sensibility. Names heard, in the sense of "listened to," are soul-making.

> Words present us with clear and familiar little pictures of things like the pictures hung on the walls of schools to give children an example of what a workbench is, a bird, an anthill, things conceived of as similar to all others of the same sort. But names present a confused image of people—and of towns, which they accustom us to believe are individual, unique, like people—an image which derives from them, from the brightness or darkness of their tone, the color with which it is painted uniformly, like one of those posters, entirely blue or entirely red, in which, because of the limitation of the process used or by a whim of the designer, not only the sky and the sea are blue or entirely red, but the boats, the church, the people in the streets.[2]

Balbec, on the coast of Normandy, where the young Marcel in the book went on holiday as an adolescent with his family, is one such name in the novel—a name we become familiar with. I have never been there, and yet, through Proust's words, it is dearer to me, more memorable to me, and better known to me, than many places I have been and did not like as much.

> As for Balbec, it was one of those names in which, as on an old piece of Norman pottery that still keeps the color of the earth from which it is fashioned, one sees depicted still the representation of some long-established custom, of some feudal right, of the former condition of some place, of an obsolete way of pronouncing the language, which had shaped and wedded its incongruous syllables and which I never doubted that I should find spoken there at once, even by the inn-keeper who would pour me out coffee and milk on my arrival, taking me down to watch the turbulent sea, unchained, before the church; to whom I lent the aspect, disputatious, solemn and medieval, of some character in one of the old romances.[3]

Names unleash fantasy. This involves, though, real reading of them and listening to them. We have to allow them to conjure up for us all that they carry of unconscious national and ancestral and historic, and imaginative, memory. Names are not made up but are conferred. An example would be naming our children. Parents "try out" in their mind possible names, taking months sometimes to decide, imaginatively exploring all the resonances and meaning of the name being considered. Often they find they cannot decide upon a name simply because they become so "carried away" by all the imaginative connotations and possibilities any name calls up. And they can talk about it for hours and hours. This is often people's first experience of the aura of names since childhood, when, invariably, names had aura, often stronger than the object; for example, "vegetable" for a young child that would not, without vigorous protest, have one on her plate; even then, its presence on the plate may contaminate the whole of the rest of what is on it, so that it all becomes uneatable. And to the frustration of the parent, the child has never even tasted the vegetable; and if they were to do so, the parent contends, they may even like it. But, for the child, the aura of the name is enough. Or the aura of "mummy" and "daddy" is stronger than almost any damage these actual personages may commit. And so on. All this is metaphysical experience and enchantment.

"I myself have had a similar experience with such names," says Adorno, rather endearingly, given that, as a philosopher, he is an unrelenting heavyweight.

> When one is on holiday as a child and reads or hears names like Monbrunn, Reuenthal, Hambrunn, one has the feeling: if only one were there, at that place, that would be it. This "it"—that the "it" is—is extraordinarily difficult to say; one will probably be able to say, following Proust's tracks here too, that is happiness. When one later reaches such places, it is not there either, one does not find "it." Often they are just foolish villages. If there is still a single stable door open in them and a smell of a real live cow and dung and such things, to which this experience is no doubt attached, one must be very thankful today. But the curious thing is that, even if "it" is not there, if one does not find in Monbrunn any of the fulfillment that is stored up in its name, nevertheless, one is not disappointed.[4]

And sometimes one finds more that "it." I did when I went straight to Jerusalem as a young man. I found infinitely more than I could have imagined. So much so that many years later, having not had the opportunity to go back, and living too far away, I still thrive on the name. I am still enchanted.

Adorno finishes his little account referring to the experience of arriving and not finding "it":

> At such moments one has a curious feeling that something is receding—rather than that one has really been done out of it. I would say, therefore, that happiness—and there is an extremely deep constellation between metaphysical experience and happiness—is something within objects and, at the same time, remote from them.

So long as names exist, and people to say them, there can be poetry after Auschwitz.

As for metaphysical experience and happiness, the word "enchantment," I think, includes happiness. But not in the Aristotelian sense, which is, at the same time, self-satisfied, or at least self-standing, conscious that "this is happiness." Such a consciousness of happiness is reification—its distortion into a quantifiable "something." The happiness in the word "enchantment" has to do with "being transported." Enchanted, we find suddenly we are not where we thought we were, and where we thought we were is not where we thought it was, or even *what* we thought it was. It is a pleasant disorientation. It is not that one is enraptured or ecstatic. It is like setting out to see the town, getting lost and ending up in fascinating parts of the town you had no idea of, but which are infinitely more interesting than what you had planned to see. Or it is like taking the wrong turn in the art gallery and, instead of seeing what you had gone to see, discovering rooms full of paintings that change your vision forever. When I first went to Rome, I walked, starting from Garibaldi's statue, and I ended up walking around cobbled streets with amazing buildings and hidden churches and squares like something out of this world. I did not see any of the "sights," but I had a time to cherish, an enchanted afternoon. Suddenly we can find ourselves transported, in the enchanted place. Such metaphysical experience *falls*.

And yet, we need to put ourselves in the way of it. Enchantment, as the name suggests, is a delicate business. Too heavy-handed, too noisy, and nothing happens. Too insouciant and laissez-faire, and nothing happens either. You cannot work to gain it any more than you can buy your way into heaven; on the other hand, if one is passive and inactive, nothing happens. Reading, listening, and gazing, all three involve deliberation, doing something about them, and then finding out, and then enjoying and learning. It is best if one can learn to read and listen and gaze in the sense we have been discussing (not the facile sense) with friends. If people who know more than we do can induct us into all that it involves and if we can talk it through with them, then all the better. Friendship based around reading, listening, and gazing is soul-making. We cannot earn enchantment or achieve it, but we do have to put ourselves in the way of it. We do so, to begin with, by attracting it, that is, by imagining it. I did not just go to Jerusalem: I imagined it for years before going there. And on the other side of the scale, the mistake I did not realize I was making in coming to Australia was that I had no imagination of it. For such lack of imagination, when it comes to life decisions, we pay a great price. Often we put it down to other "causes" and do not realize, actually, that it had to do with lack of enchantment. And, anyway, who is there to enlighten us? Enchantment is hardly understood.

Young Marcel in *Remembrance of Things Past* is too poorly to be sent by his parents to stay at Balbec, but he imagines taking the train there, "so as to become acquainted with the architecture and landscapes of Normandy and Brittany, that one twenty-two train into which I had so often clambered in imagination, I should have preferred to stop, and to alight from it, as at the most beautiful of its towns; but in vain might I compare and contrast them; how was one to choose, any more than between individual people, who are not interchangeable, between Bayeux, so lofty in its noble coronet of rusty lace, whose highest point caught the light of the old gold of its second syllable; Vitré, whose acute accent barred its ancient glass with wooden lozenges; gentle Lamballe, whose whiteness ranged from egg-shell yellow to a pearly grey; Coutances, a Norman Cathedral, which its final consonants, rich and yellowing, crowned with a tower of butter; Lannion with the rumble and buzz, in the silence of its village street, of the fly on the wheel of the coach; Questambert, Pontorson, ridiculously silly and simple, white feathers and yellow beaks strewn along the road to those well-watered and poetic spots; Benodet, a name scarcely moored that seemed to be striving to draw the river down into the tangle of its seaweeds; Pont Aven, the snowy, rosy flight of the wing of a lightly poised coif, tremulously reflected in the greenish waters of a canal; Quimperlé, more firmly attached, this, and since the Middle Ages, among the rivulets with which it babbled, threading their pearls upon a grey background, like the pattern made, through the cobwebs upon a window, by rays of sunlight changed into blunt points of tarnished silver?"[5]

We all have our place-names. The Cotswolds, outside Oxford, where I am from, was all that was meant by "the countryside" so that every book set in the countryside that I read, from *The Country Child* by Alison Uttley, in primary school, to *The Woodlanders* by Thomas Hardy, later on, in secondary school, was set there, although *The Country Child* is set in Shropshire and the Hardy novels in a fictional Wessex, which corresponds to Wiltshire, Devonshire, and nearby counties; so I knew that more lustrous and wonderful countryside existed beyond the Cotswolds, which were too homely for Hardy, as even these words "homely" and Hardy already tell us. And the family Sunday afternoon drives into the countryside were continuous with this imaginative experience. From the book to the place was no distance; sight reinforced imagination and vice versa. In Wantage, where King Alfred "who burnt the cakes" came from, we would stop for something to eat. I never knew why he burnt the cakes but supposed he was in a hurry to escape; although, upon reflection now, I can see he would then have abandoned the cakes: but to me, then, it seemed unquestionable that Alfred burnt the cakes there in Wantage because he was in a hurry to escape his enemies. I took it for granted that kings always had enemies. And it always felt to me as though King Alfred was still hiding somewhere about the town. There were buildings with his name on them, like the old pub, and he could quite well be in one of those. I never needed to enquire which century King Alfred belonged to (it was the ninth!) because I knew it was our own. This is how metaphysical experience works, if we are lucky; and I was. The Cotswolds too was an area associated, no doubt, with early memories of my uncle's farm, which had cows, sheep, pigs, dogs, a hay barn, roosters, and deep mud—everything a farm, before agribusiness, could be expected to contain. And, imaginatively, the Cotswolds remains for me an Arcadia that I can remember like yesterday; and I am pleased that I can remember it in all four seasons. As for the names of Cotswolds villages...for me they are irremediably associated with the enchantment of childhood: Hook Norton; Duns Tew and Little Tew; Deddington; Banbury, famous for its Cross in the market square; Burford; Bourton-on-the-water, which was my favorite because the clear running shallow stream bore the sky with it and its huge smooth flat pebbles felt beautifully cool to hot little feet. Every name was picturesque in its own way.

On the other hand, the name of London eclipsed all other names, for it was a proper city (whatever that meant, but I knew what it meant without thinking about it). London was always unaccommodating, like a hard heavy stone, and sounded powerful, but also London meant the stone of battlements, of castle walls, of borders, kingdoms, and of empire (a word which was, for some reason, a little frightening, for it meant having to leave, by ship of course, and go far away forever). London meant bigger, older, and richer, where the Queen lived in Buckingham Palace, and where they had real criminals such as I had seen in television serializations of Dickens. For me, London is always Dickensian, for even my experience of modern London when I revisit is filtered through Dickens, just as Salisbury and Winchester, where my cousins live, is filtered, when I am actually there, through Trollope's fictional Barsetshire. And beyond the provincial market towns of fictional Barsetshire, if you go out in the country, say to Shaftesbury or Tisbury or down toward Plymouth and get stuck in the moors, Exmoor and Dartmoor, it is possible to die of exposure—and there is a special prison there, I was told, for mad people and murderers. I saw it from a distance once, a monolith of old stone with peep-hole windows and a wall. Then I am out of Trollope's Barsetshire; I am in Thomas Hardy's fictional Wessex, which is deeply green, between towering hedgerows and endless windy lanes that recall the walking tracks they once were, or where it suddenly breaks out barren and lonely on the moors, and where life is more rural and remote and rough than the towns of Barsetshire. As for Malmsbury or Glastonbury...I feel closer to another world in these spots. Joseph of Arimathea, who paid for the tomb where they laid the dead Jesus, had come to Glastonbury in the first century; and that oriental connection seems still to linger about the place. A descendant of the tree he planted is still there, not even fenced off, just with a plaque, so far as I recall along the lines of, "Joseph of Arimathea planted this tree. Please Do Not Touch..." A masterpiece of English understatement. But perhaps it has changed since my last visit.

With enchantment it is impossible to tell "fiction" and "reality" apart. They merely reinforce each other. Enchanted, we walk around in the past rather than the present, which does not really exist as such because, in all the great places of the earth, it simply cannot. When I left home I went to live in Jerusalem for a few years; now *there* is a place where the present is *palpably* the living past. To me that is why it is holy.

We all have our resonances with place-names and it a soul-making exercise to recall them, for our enchantment is wrapped up with them. Reading Proust, we learn to resonate again with metaphysical experience, and if we can read Proust's work for all its worth, then too, we experience enchantment.

We may extend what we have said about place-names to naming words generally. Words have resonances, and these "resonances" refer to something happening within the unison of our inner sensibility and sensitivity, our soul.

We may just take one more example from Proust. Young Marcel is out for a walk with his father and grandfather near their home in the village of Combray. They have taken a route along the grounds of the home where Monsieur Swann and his wife, formerly Odette de Crécy, live, and are admiring the flowering pink hawthorn growing there.

> Suddenly I stopped, I could not move, as happens when something we see does not merely address our eyes, but requires a deeper kind of perception and possesses our entire being. A little girl with reddish blonde hair, who appeared to be coming back from a walk and held a gardening spade in her hand, was looking at us, lifting towards us a face scattered with pink freckles.[6]

This is young Marcel's first sight of the girl who will be his first love.

> I looked at her, at first with the sort of gaze that is not merely the messenger of the eyes, but a window at which all the senses lean out, anxious and petrified, a gaze that would touch the body it is looking at, capture it, take it away and the soul along with it...

Seeing young Marcel's father and grandfather, "she turned away and with an indifferent and disdainful look, placed herself at an angle to spare her face from being in their field of vision." Then as they passed, behind their backs, she gazed back at Marcel, "at full length in my direction, without any particular expression, without appearing to see me." But she must have seen him, for she seems to have smiled secretly to herself and "at the same time her hand sketched an indecent gesture."

> —Gilberte, come here! What are you doing? came the piercing, authoritarian cry of a lady in white whom I had not seen...

The name!

So it was that this name Gilberte passed by close to me, given to me like a talisman that might enable me to find her again, this girl whom it had just turned into a person and who, a moment before, had been merely an uncertain image. So it passed, spoken over the jasmines and the stocks, as sour and as cool as the drops from the green watering hose; impregnating, coloring the portion of pure air that it had crossed—and that it isolated—with the mystery of the life of the girl that it designated...

And so they pass each other by. "And already the charm with which the incense of her name had imbued that place under the pink hawthorns where it had been heard by her and me together, was beginning to reach, to overlay, to perfume everything that came near it, her grandparents, whom my own had had the ineffable happiness of knowing, the sublime profession of stockbroker, the harrowing neighborhood of the Champs-Élysées where she lived in Paris."

We filter out our experience in our social contexts today because this is how we learn and how we are taught, so that names mean next to nothing beyond their "function" to designate this or that. Proust, here, retrieves the truth of the real presence of words and names in particular. It is not merely as if Mrs. Swann calls her daughter's name, as is in fact the case, but to one more deeply attentive, the girl's name is called as if Adam himself had called it, as in the biblical story where Adam gives all things their names. As Proust says, the name turned the image into a person, and now the person may be present, by virtue of their name, where in fact they are absent; for instance, if Marcel's parents are to talk about Gilberte at home. The girl's presence is suddenly everywhere around in the world, perfuming everything, as Proust has it.

Of course we can take other examples, such as dreaded names. Then there are legendary names that come down through history and are timeless in the sense that they keep reverberating in one period of time after another. But, today, this sense of the importance of names for our inner sensibility, our soul, is narrowed to the nuclear family. Then there are the famous names bandied about in the media. But what is such fame? In Rilke, "Fame, after all, is but the sum of all the misunderstandings which gather around a new name."[7] Fame is categorically impersonal and depersonalizing, which is why, if one is sensitive and soulful *and* famous, fame can be destructive. Some names, pronounced between us, Rilke also says, may establish a friendship and cordiality and unanimity.[8] These are important names.

Since Rilke's day, or Proust's, the world has changed, not in a natural or organic way, but it has been forced to change by powerful ideological interests, predominantly those of big capitalism, and now our world is infested and teeming with innumerable improper names, which are on everyone's tongues, such as all those of which we have initialisms or acronyms, and "brand" names, all of which harness the power of the proper name for "economic" interests. Too few people in such a world realize the importance of names and can therefore regret the level of disenchantment brought about by the loss of proper names and their replacement by jargon, by technical language, professionalized language, brands, and initialisms; or the replacement of proper names by the dumb silence of those mindlessly occupied with staring at screens and playing some "game" or "messaging." The loss of proper names marks the loss of sensitivity and sensibility within us and of the wonderful aura within which every name resonates. But unless we read Proust or some other author of his ilk, how can we know better?

Notes

1. For further reading, see Daniel Barenboim, *Everything is Connected: The Power of Music* (London: George Weidenfeld & Nicholson, 2008), 1–23, 45–59.
2. Proust, "The Way by Swann's," 391.
3. Proust, *Swann's Way*, Part Two, 236.
4. Adorno, *Metaphysics*, 464.
5. Proust, *Swann's Way*, Part One, 236f.
6. Proust, "The Way by Swann's," 141ff.
7. Rainer Maria Rilke, *Rodin and Other Pieces*, trans. G. Craig Houston (London: Quartet, 1986), 3.
8. Ibid., 45.

7

Narcissus

From these considerations of enchantment in its primary colors of reading, listening, and gazing we want to further our story by turning to our second icon, as it were, or lens, through whose work we wish to discern the lineaments of enchantment yet further and embellish our *twisted secular metaphysics*. In speaking of Rilke, we must speak also of Lou Salomé, his lover and muse. Before she met Rilke, Lou had been an associate of Nietzsche, and after her affair with Rilke, although while they were still in touch by letter, Lou helped Freud at the inception of psychoanalysis. With Rilke, Lou Salomé enters our story too. Nietzsche, Rilke, and Freud are names it is customary to associate with a metaphysics of a twisted secular kind, to say the least.

This chapter and the next four chapters will be about enchantment and the work of enchantment thought through Rilke and Lou Salomé. Then our last two chapters, for completion, will concern work by Goethe. While we have moved sideways in front of the *iconostasis* and are beholding a different icon now (no longer Proust but Rilke), we have before our eyes, as we would if we were Orthodox believers in front of real icons, the same matter before our mind's eye—that of enchantment. As with Proust, so with Rilke, we shall reap a double benefit from his icon or window into enchantment, for not only what he enables us to see, but, secondly, for the fact that, as far as reading goes, the work of enchantment itself, Rilke is surely compulsory reading. As with Proust, Rilke's will be a literary work (his *Duino Elegies* are, indeed, a literary masterpiece) that invites us into another world, a world which, by virtue of entering it, we can see our own world and ourselves more clearly. Only the best of art allows for this, and that is why it is *called* the best of art: it is not merely someone's subjective imposition on the rest of us, or their private opinion being canvassed. Great art has a great effect—but only if people have the sensibility for it. Naturally we are capable of reaching the heights and depths of sensibility when we interpret all things to our communal satisfaction, but that is not to say that we necessarily do reach them. We can become occluded in our souls; and we started this book by saying, through Adorno principally, that our time suffers this occlusion, at least in part. In such a time we have all the more need for art, but we cannot have art without the work of enchantment—reading, listening, and gazing—the work on the inner sensibilities, which is part and parcel of art on the receptive end. Reading Rilke, entering his world, being captivated by his poetry, is work very much in an Enlightenment spirit. Rilke opens our sensibility and his poetry induces enchantment even while it raises the very subject itself, just as Proust's work does.

We will enter Rilke's world, and my account in this chapter and those to follow will afford some introduction to him for readers who have not heard of him before. Then, at the start of our last Rilke chapter (Chapter 11), I will recapitulate what we should have garnered up to that point about the work of enchantment, much as I did with Proust. Then we will turn to our final "icon," Goethe.

Rainer Maria Rilke is regarded as Germany's greatest lyric poet. His *Duino Elegies* (1921) are regarded as belonging to that genre invented by Goethe, in a term coined by him, and with work contributed by him (notably his *Faust* tragedy): "world literature." The *Duino Elegies* are probably, with their title, a nod to Goethe's erotic *Roman Elegies*, themselves a nod to Propertius' classic *Elegies*.

Rilke met and fell in love with Lou Salomé, who was 15 years his senior, in 1897. Twice, at the turn of the century, they visited Tolstoy in Russia. While Rilke and Lou's affair lasted just over 2 years, their spiritual bond (and famous correspondence) lasted until Rilke's death in 1926. As with Proust, I would not go into the details of Rilke's life, which may be found in an encyclopedia or other such storehouse of information very easily. But I will say a bit more about Lou, who is just as important, but less well known.[1]

Lou Salomé was the daughter of an aristocratic general in the court of Tsar Alexander II; she traveled in Europe; spoke Russian, German, French, and Italian fluently; wrote 20 books and many articles. Nietzsche's best friend, Paul Reé, was in love with her in Rome, when he wrote to Nietzsche, who he believed to be in Genoa, and asked him to join them. Nietzsche was just *turning* toward all that he would become in his own inner life and ours. He had left Genoa for Messina, where the letter eventually reached him. He caught up with Reé and Lou in Rome. He fell in love with her too. They formed a ménage-à-trois. Her idea. A "holy trinity" they called it. Nietzsche read "The Madman" aphorism to them at Rome, part of the book that he would publish as *The Gay Science*, in which, in the aphorism I am speaking of, a madman declares in the marketplace that God is dead, God remains dead, and that *we have killed him*. A capital philosophical text in the history of modern thought. Nietzsche, no womanizer, believed Lou to be his intellectual peer, and discussed his ideas with her. He proposed marriage several times, only to be rejected. Lou wrote the first book on Nietzsche's work, which is still one of the best books on Nietzsche, around whom now flourishes a whole academic publishing industry.

In 1911, Lou met Freud, a man who was rewriting philosophy in terms of the soul of the individual. Freud had discovered something people were largely unconscious of, which he called "sexuality." This quality of the soul, he thought, was definitional for what went on between people, for the points of coalescence and demarcation, for the dynamics of every relationship, and it affected inner thought including philosophical thought. Lou had already in 1910 published a book entitled *Eroticism*. She and Freud were very much on the same page, as it were. Lou was a legend in intellectual circles in Europe, including Freud's. Lou had known Nietzsche, Wagner, and Tolstoy; she knew Rilke, Strindberg, Buber, Hofmenstahl, Hauptmann, and Scheler. Her biographer writes: "A female Faust she was not interested in rummaging in empty words. She wanted to 'detect the inmost force that binds the world and guides its course,' she wanted to know it, to experience it, to live it."[2] Lou and Freud had already set their sails to the same course before they ever met. Of all the great men she met, Freud was the first who stopped Lou in her tracks. She recognized a teacher and mentor, and a reverse situation took place for the first time in her life: she fell under his spell. And he did not, like so many of the others, succumb to her charms, although he recognized and even revered her intellectual versatility and insight. She moved to Vienna and enrolled in his lectures. And then she worked with him at the inception of psychoanalysis; a student, but also a colleague, she helped to bring Freud's soulful science about.

According to her 1910 book *Eroticism*, Lou speaks of Narcissus as a germinal soul-story as, at the core of narcissism, there is a tension between self-love and self-surrender. In the Greek myth, Narcissus looks into the water, looks into the depths. He sees his reflection gaze back at him rather than the depths; he sees not just himself, but the trees and the sky—nature, in short. He sees his own face and sees it in nature. He does not just see himself, but himself against the backdrop of nature.

Lou asks: "Does not his face express melancholy as well as enchantment?" Enchantment, because he is delighted with what he sees, especially with the sight of himself. Melancholy, because he is estranged from what he sees; he senses his exile, even with regard to himself.

This is important. Enchantment is coupled with melancholy.

Melancholy is the mood in which the soul is made ready to become sensitized. Melancholy "opens" the soul, lays it bare. Melancholy, we are sensitive. We are not sad, we are not despondent. These are a different music. We are not depressed. Then we cannot hear the music. Melancholy is none of these. We do not induce melancholy either. As the poet Keats says, in his famous *Ode on Melancholy*, "But when a melancholy fit shall fall/ Sudden from heaven like a weeping cloud..." Melancholy *falls*, and from heaven. In other words, it is good, beneficent, and heaven-sent. It moistens the soul, like soil is moistened if what is rooted there should grow. But here, what is to grow is our inwardness. Melancholy is a mood we fall into. It takes us by surprise. It "takes" us, in the full biblical sense of the ravished bride that is "taken." In Freud's language melancholy is sexual, in the sense of a general unawakened languishing as a ground-mood of existence—in contrast to awakened sexuality, which is creative and wants to give birth. In ordinary language, melancholy is a mood. But it is not a mood in the temperamental sense in which, perhaps, I wake up "on the wrong side of the bed" in a bad mood; or, alternatively, in which, "I am happy as Larry." Melancholy is a ground-mood in the sense that, according to the philosopher Martin Heidegger, anxiety and boredom are, because the way we "deal" with time opens out from these ground-moods, or closes back into them if we are not careful. A ground-mood is a mood as close as possible or as imaginable to the experience of our naked being or to the intimacy of our solitude. A ground-mood is a basic condition of "experience." Melancholy does not center the self but opens it for the possibility of determination, and melancholy has the effect of making the self extremely vulnerable. This is when, if the mind is like antennae, the antennae are at a fever pitch of receptivity.[3]

Melancholy is also, traditionally, related to our exile. In this world we know what ought to be the case: justice and mercy. And we can see we exist apart from a world where these reign. As Levinas puts it: "And love means, before all else, the welcoming of the other as *thou*. Can that welcome be carried out empty-handed?"[4] We know what heaven is like: it is a place of harmony where good prevails; and we know this earth is not like that: "And after this our exile" said T.S. Eliot, who recalled all this about melancholy and exile in *Ash Wednesday, 1930* so perfectly. We know our job (if we know anything) is to make this world conform more to how things *ought* to be. And yet we get sidetracked and forget, or stuck in a never-ending argument. Even relations in our own world are a mess and their fate, perhaps, out of our control; how much more impossible other relationships then! Melancholy is related to realism. Every realistic novel is a melancholy affair and every death-bed scene.

Melancholy can easily sink to darker, more confining moods, which are not from heaven. To avoid this dire fate we must know what the poets and artists down the ages have to tell us. This is what the humanities used to teach. If we sink into darker moods we cannot become initiated into the beauty, depth, joy, and aching pleasure that the melancholy fit portends.

Enchantment presupposes melancholy, as Lou Salomé perhaps was first to theorize in her work on the erotic, and as Rilke would show in his poetry. We are not really part of things in the sense of "that openness that is so deep in the animal's vision," as Rilke wrote, for "we never have that pure space in front of us, nor for a single day, such as flowers open endlessly into" (Eighth Elegy).[5] Self-love and self-surrender at the heart of our being—our "sexuality"—confines us within the world, within the human. "Always," Rilke wrote, for us "there is world, and never the Nowhere without the Not: the pure/ unwatched-over, that one breathes and endlessly knows, without craving" (Eighth Elegy). We will look more deeply into Rilke's Elegies later.

Melancholy is a ground-mood because it is the state in which we will strengthen the unison that deepens our inner sensibility and sensitivity, and because it is the precondition for soul-work and soul-making.

In an evil situation, melancholy is impossible. In suffering and attrition, melancholy is impossible. Melancholy is anything but dark. It is like that November light in northern Europe, so still, in which the spring, the summer, and the autumn seem to be invisibly gathered and remembered. Therefore in situations of injustice, in unjust societies, there are imperatives that come before melancholy. The human stage must be set for soul-work. There must be freedom. But on the other hand, the happy cannot be melancholy. Happiness is oblivious to others and set on itself. The happy are not soul-workers any more than those who are sufferers—and perhaps even less so.

Soul-work therefore occurs within a median band of experience. It cannot abide extremes. Enchantment is only possible where melancholy can *fall*, which is not anywhere and not everywhere.

Notes

1. For further reading on Rilke, first see Lou's book: Lou Andreas-Salomé, *You Alone Are Real to Me: Remembering Rainer Maria Rilke*, trans. Angela von der Lippe (Manchester: Carcenet, 2004), written just after Rilke's death in 1927 and originally published simply as *Rainer Maria Rilke* (Leipzig: Insel, 1928). See also Stephanie Dowrick, *In the Company of Rilke* (Sydney: Allen & Unwin, 2009). The long subtitle of this book, which reveals something about the author's interpretation of Rilke, is: *Why a 20th-Century Visionary Poet Speaks So Eloquently to 21st-Century Readers Yearning for Inwardness, Beauty & Spiritual Connection.*

       She does not see the dark side of Rilke as much as I do. Nevertheless, it is a deeply experienced book in terms of my thesis about enchantment.
2. H.F. Peters, *My Sister, My Spouse: A Biography of Lou Andreas-Salomé* (New York: Norton, 1962), 12.
3. See my *The Valley Way of Soul: Melancholy, Poetry, and Soul-Making* (Sydney: St Pauls, 2008), 41–49.
4. Levinas, *Proper Names*, 5–6.
5. All excerpts from the Elegies in this chapter are from the translation by A.S. Kline (2001), with gracious permission of the translator. <http://www.poetryintranslation.com> (accessed January 2, 2010).

8

Narcissus Later

Later, after Lou had become involved with Freud in Vienna, Rilke wrote down a poem for her at Loufried, her home in Göttingen, which she shared with her husband, the Orientalist, Carl Andreas. The poem, dated July 20, 1913, was entitled *Narcissus*. Along with this he wrote out and gave her a copy of the poem "Mary's Death," from his *Life of Mary* (1912). Lou pasted the pages into her diary.[1]

Narcissus is a perfect poem for the two of them who both gauged this tension within themselves of the need, bodily, for self-preservation and retaining, and of the need for largesse, generosity, giving. They were both "narcissists," both creators, both soul-workers, both destructive of others, both enchanters therefore. These two needs, or "drives," as Freud would later call them, do not rest in peace, and yet, from them, Rilke evokes something charming to read, which is soul-making—if we can read it! For this is not a matter of reading the words, but through the words, to imaginatively ascertain and re-live that experience; and so to touch the narcissism within ourselves, this tension of a double bind in which we are caught, always; just as we also always struggle to release ourselves. So much "spirituality," by contrast, issues from an inflation of this double tension into all sorts of religious concepts, such as compassion or love, which, as concepts, may operate falsely, aside from experience. Rilke, rather than inflating the experience spiritually, and taking it beyond the bounds of knowing, condenses the experience so much that reading it is a task that may require a lengthy inception and preparation. We are unused to this kind of reading. But this is reading as the work of enchantment.

At first, Narcissus loses himself in the image he beholds. The poem begins with his diffusion:

> And so this: this emanates from me and dissolves
> in the air and in the aura of the grove,
> leaves me gently and becomes something mine no longer
> and gleams because it meets no enmity.

Let the words resound like charms in your soul to let them communicate their meaning there. Rilke's words "because it meets no enmity" speak the lack of tension, the release that keeps releasing. Yet, more deeply, within the poem, within the words, Narcissus strains toward union as one does in the heterosexual act:

> What forms there and so resembles me
> and quivers upward in tear-stained signals,—
> *it perhaps took shape just this way*
> *inside a woman; it was beyond attaining*
> *(however hard I struggled for it pressing into her).*
> Now it lies open in the indifferent
> scattered water, and I may gaze at it
> no end beneath my wreath of roses.

Rilke's underlining, in his manuscript, of the words set here in italics, underlines an urgent effort toward union: "pressing into her" has many levels, from the obvious, to a more psychic pressing in, which would destroy the other inwardly, by invading the other with oneself, rather than, as in the sexual-physical sense, enable procreation. Narcissus cannot procreate; that is his frustration and defeat, although everything he sees is procreative.

We have said that Narcissus wanted to look into the depths. He saw the surfaces. Everything is open and before us "in the indifferent scattered water." The depth is phantasmal:

It is not loved there. Down there is nothing
but the equanimity of tumbled stones,
and I can see my sadness.

In other words, what we are saying here is that Rilke captured for Lou her own theory, described in *Eroticism*, about the narcissistic nature of the erotic, which, Freud will elaborate, is a dimension of all relationship. (Of course, by contrast, the English notion of the erotic is narrow, a narrowing itself emblematic of constricting and walled-in souls.) Rilke's poetry dismantles those walls, whether they are prisons or defenses. Reading it—really reading it (and later, we shall)—dismantles those walls, and what we will experience upon release is "enchantment."

Lou and Rilke were both narcissists. That is why he was potentially destructive for Lou, and, after a couple of years of him as her lover, she realized that, for her own self-preservation, she must keep her distance. And so their relationship moved into one of correspondence. There is something about correspondence which is important to note, especially in our age of instant and banal "communications." Correspondences have their own time. They exist in a different time from that which we measure on our watches and clocks, our calculated and quantified time. Correspondences, at least of this type between Lou and Rilke, exist in a qualitative dimension of reflective time, of inner time, of inner sensitivity and sensibility, of soul-time. This time is immeasurable. Only by a serious correspondence, such as that between Lou and Rilke, which is so much more than a so-called "love story in letters," can we enter into this kind of time. Also, reading the letters, we can enter their time. Lou's correspondence with Rilke is exemplary, but her correspondence with Freud is not of the same kind. We have to read Kafka's correspondence with Regina to find something at all comparable in terms of the intensity of this experience of time and in terms of giving us access to such experience. In this sense, the correspondence belongs to art, to their art, as much as to their other writings. Today, because of the communications industry, which straddles and dominates the world, and flings humans into a mad rush of assorted connections and "networks," as we say, correspondence has gone by the board and, with it, this sense of another time, of time and being, of immeasurable time. Instead, nearly everyone is bound to follow the same time where, essentially, money is the meaning of time. For Lou and Rilke, we can say, rightly, that love is the meaning of time, but it is more than love. Lou is Rilke's muse, his mistress, his older sister (not his mother figure, as some have said). She is his analyst before the inception of psychoanalysis. To read their correspondence is great reading, real reading, soul-work, preparation for reading the poems, of which the great Elegies are the hardest to read of all.

Rilke's narcissism was destructive, and, alone, living in the Château de Muzot above Sierre (Valais) in Switzerland, the destruction was wrought within, in the essential tension we have just described, which he infinitely *risked*:

We, we infinitely risked...[2]

Why infinitely? the critic Maurice Blanchot asks. And answers: "Man is the most precarious of beings, for he jeopardizes everything."[3]

For as I lose myself to my own gaze:
I could think that I am deadly.

Words so truly spoken, how could Rilke have known? For he would die before long of a disease of the blood. And Rilke, like Nietzsche, linked writing to the blood in the writer's veins. In the *Notebook of Malte Laurids Brigge*, Rilke wrote—what applied in the book but also applied to himself—that, before we write, experiences must "have turned to blood within us."[4]

Rilke's knowledge was what Lou called "dark knowledge,"[5] ever recollective of death; and his enchantment is indeed a dark rapture. In the Elegies, a dark rapture, but elsewhere too, leading up to them, his enchantment (which we, his readers, come to share) is an expressive quality that, according to Lou, made him a first-rate storyteller "and made him able to transform even the most simple impressions and experiences into a unique and unforgettable event."[6] Rilke wrote to Lou from Paris (June 26, 1914):

> I am like a little anemone that I once saw in my garden in Rome. It had opened up so wide during the day that it could not close during the night! It was terrible to see it in the dark meadow, wide open, still inhaling everything through its wide-open throat—with the much too imposing night above that would not be consumed. And nearby, the clever sisters, each closed around its small body. I too am incurably exposed and vulnerable.[7]

In January 1912:

> How often it happens that I emerge like chaos from my room and I am seized by the presence of an outsider. I discover a style that actually belongs to that other. And in the next moment, to my astonishment, I articulate things so beautifully, while everything in my consciousness was completely amorphous.[8]

During the war Rilke could write nothing. His amorphous openness, his receptivity, his soulfulness, would only increase, much to his pain. He had married the artist Clara Westhoff in 1901, and he was a father (Ruth was born the same year); he had obligations, but these did not prevent him sacrificing them (by abandoning them) to follow his artistic bent. Lou's superb memoir, written in 1927, the year after his death, focuses on Rilke the artist, not the lover, husband or father. It is not a biography. Yet it is more than a memoir: it is actually the completion of Rilke's work, the capstone on it, what he would have written, had he been her, which he tried to be, but could never be. Lou's memoir of Rilke is what one of Rilke's angels would have written; but we shall have reason to reflect on those angels later. Rilke's "openness" led him to solitude and to a narcissistic intimacy, where the tension between self-love and self-sacrifice would tear his body asunder from his soul, so great was its intensity.

Notes

1. See both poems together in context in *Rilke and Andreas-Salomé: A Love Story in Letters*, ed. Edward Snow and Michael Winkler (New York: W.W. Norton, 2006), 210-11. (Henceforth: Rilke and Salomé, *Letters*)
2. Rilke, *Sonnets to Orpheus*, II. 24, cited by Maurice Blanchot, *The Space of Literature*, trans. Ann Smock (Lincoln/London: University of Nebraska Press, 1989), 236.

3. Blanchot, *The Space of Literature*, 236–7.
4. Rilke, *The Notebook of Malte Laurids Brigge*, trans. John Linton (London: Hogarth Press, 1959), 20.
5. Salomé, *You Alone Are Real to Me*, 89.
6. Ibid., 61.
7. Ibid., 80.
8. Ibid., 81.

9

The Turning

Enchantment is always enchainment. Enchainment is to our proper destiny or calling, or the difference which we are here to make; this destiny or difference is what pulls us, and keeps pulling us, in a particular direction and one day becomes our story. That is the path of enchantment for each of us. But only by virtue of enchantment does our enchainment become our enthrallment. For Rilke, this destiny was especially enthralling because he was to become a poet of the first order. As a top-rank poet, his job would be to disclose something to the rest of us, to enthrall us in turn, if there is anyone left to hear. Of this, Rilke was not too certain. But he knew Lou could hear, and not just hear, but listen.

On the morning of June 20, 1914, a date on the brink of the collapse of Europe and the thousand-year-old Austro-Hungarian empire, he wrote a poem called *The Turning* and sent it to Lou. The poem was not about the imminent end of Europe, but about himself. Narcissus again. And yet, in being about himself, he wrote words that belonged on the other side of the catastrophe, not to the time which was catastrophic. August 1914, the start of the First World War; Europe would not recover. The Second World War was almost a denouement of the lack of settlement in Europe, the level of "unfinished business" among nations and peoples. But Rilke's words chimed beyond these horizons—and, perhaps, even beyond our own. For haven't we entered an unprecedented time of war? Aren't we still in it?

The Turning is about the emergence of what it is to be Rilke.[1] Lou was the first, before Rilke, to realize this. She was the rational one. This was not just a poem called *The Turning*; this was a turning point for Rilke, a turning point for his destiny. *The Turning* finds its consummation in the *Duino Elegies*, started around this time, and finished in February 1922.

In an epigraph to *The Turning*, Rilke cites Kassner.

"The path from inner intensity to greatness leads through sacrifice." Rilke would have to live these words, and I think he did.

In a word, the poem is about *gazing*—about the transformation of soul wrought through gazing.

> He had long prevailed through gazing.
> Stars fell to their knees
> under his grappling up-glance.
> Or he gazed kneeling,
> and the scent of his urgency
> lulled a Force immortal,
> until it smiled on him from sleep.
> Towers he gazed at with such force
> that they were startled...

The poem continues as a gaze.

Rilke's gaze is not of this world but of the world to come, a world beyond the European wars all around him, even though he wrote in the break. A world beyond the rape of the earth by state socialism with its big industry, and commodity capitalism with its encroaching technology. Rilke's poetry is already the poetry of this world to come; in this sense, his poetry is "not of this world" any more than he was. His turning is in a sense yet to be determined (yet *where* might it be determined?) by the turning of we who gaze, listen, and read.

Lou, who normally does not write to Rilke at anywhere near the same length that she writes to him when she receives this poem, writes straight back. "I am so *fully* in company of your words and with them alone."[2] And she replies in a heartfelt way, trying to reflect

Rilke's achievement back to him, because she knows he knows that she alone is capable of this. She goes on to work with him the whole way to the Elegies.

Rilke's turning marks a reassessment of all values. When this happens, as occasionally it must, at axial times, it happens silently, far from the fleas of the marketplace.[3] Lou, of course, knew this as well as Rilke.

Lou sends another letter to Rilke a couple of days later. Even to her soulfulness, which was optimal—for she was a wise enchantress, a muse, a genius of a sort not recognized by public prizes—Rilke's poem had taken a while to *fall*.

> It was only after my letter to you had gone off a few days ago that I began to live with the *poem itself*; I couldn't do so at first because its personal immediacy had overwhelmed me too thoroughly. And now I read, or more accurately: say it out loud to myself again and again.[4]

She realizes that this poem *is* what it says. It is a turning indeed, and in how many ways? In how many directions? She cannot say. But:

> Somewhere in this realm, deep down, all art *begins* again with renewed force, arises as from its primordial origin, where it was magic formula, incantation,—a calling forth of life in its still concealed mysteriousness,—yes, where it was at once prayer and the most intense breaking-forth of power.
>
> I do not tire of contemplating this.[5]

These are dramatic words of realization. She cannot fully foresee the consequences of what he has written, of what he will now write, and she will read. Neither can he. Neither can we. This book now, in fact, is part of the consequences of that poem, then. But she could feel the Elegies coming. So could he. And now we have them. They are ours to *read*. But we need to read them aloud (yes, even translations of them) as well as to listen to them, as well as to read them silently to ourselves, and see if we can see and hear what they transfigure.

And later, we will come to the Elegies, to read them for their *dark enchantment*.

On reading *The Turning*, Lou turned back to the poem *Narcissus*, which Rilke had written for her the year before.

This gazing that *The Turning* speaks of is narcissistic. But the poem, says Rilke, has reached the edge of the narcissistic gaze.

Work of the eyes is done,
begin heart-work now
on those images in you, those captive ones;
for you conquered them: but you still don't know them.

Lou knew that for Rilke "Art is the *dark wish* of all things. They want to be the images of our secrets..."[6] What Lou realized with *The Turning* is that this art, this "heart-work," was to be lived and embodied. In her memoir of Rilke, she wrote, "Rilke perceived his corporeality as just such an awkward abode; it was that aspect of the self that could not be subsumed in the creative process. As such, it represented, in no ascetic or moral sense, an opposing force, a threat. It embraces the creative principle, even if it is not interchangeable with the other."[7] But she wrote this years later. It was in 1914 that this became apparent to her, for in her letter to him, she shows that she is aware that he is turning because he is about to embrace the creative principle bodily.

> This running up against the inorganic, this becoming doll, in other words, this running up against our body, which for us (even though it is organic life) is yet the outermost outside in its most intimate sense, the first partition that differentiates us from ourselves, makes us the "inner being" lodged in it like the face in a hedgehog; our very body, with its hands, feet, eyes, ears, all the parts we enumerate as "us"; this perplexing tangle generally unfurls only in response to the loving comportment of an other, who alone legitimates, in a manner we can bear, our body as "us." In a "creative person" though, the components perpetually loosen and renew their ties: which is why, instead of repetition, new reality emanates from him.

You are in pain: I, through your pain, feel bliss.
Forgive me for that.

She believed that the *eros* of Rilke's poems—his Elegies, as it would turn out—would be bisexual, for at the heart of Narcissus, and the tension we have noted, is the clash of a dual sexuality within us, which is creative. We need to be careful here not to confuse the post-1960s "liberationist" ideas of bisexuality (as self-indulgence or self-expression) with what Lou is talking about. The latter version stands in relation to what she is talking about as *kitsch* does to art; or, in a more Rilkean comparison, as mass-produced things stand in relation to those things generations old, loved, and handed down to us by our forebears. For Lou, the investiture of the external form, the exertion of power is "the masculine moment" of creativity; the feminine moment is the power by which one surrenders to one's art, to one's lover; it is a longing for pregnancy.[8] Rilke, in his creativity, was going to take both forms of power together, which, elsewhere, we have called the melancholy and the enchanting.

His pain is our bliss. All true art is a service for all on behalf of all, the artist obliging him—or herself before all others.

Notes

1. The whole poem may be seen in context in Rilke and Salomé, *Letters*, 243-4. The original title is "Wendung."
2. Rilke and Salomé, *Letters*, 245.
3. Friedrich Nietzsche, *Thus Spoke Zarathustra*, trans. Walter Kaufmann (London/New York: Penguin, 1978), 51-2.
4. Rilke and Salomé, *Letters*, 246.
5. Ibid., 246-7.
6. Salomé, *You Alone Are Real to Me*, 95.
7. Ibid., 64.
8. See Lou's discussion in *You Alone Are Real to Me*, 54-5.

10

Dark Enchantment

After the turning, Rilke was spiritually capable of continuing, indeed of completing, something he had started, which as yet had no shape: the work which came to be known as the *Duino Elegies*. He had begun these in 1912 at Castle Duino on the Adriatic coast, the home of a patroness, Princess Marie Thurn-und-Taxis-Hohenloe, one of Europe's richest women. The war would interrupt him. After the war, he continued to work and parts of the Elegies, as he was calling them, came in fits and spurts. But in February 1922, at Château Muzot, his borrowed home in Switzerland, he finished the 10 Elegies and 55 *Sonnets to Orpheus*. One of the greatest poetic achievements of the twentieth century was born into the world.

On 11 February, in the evening, he wrote to Lou:

Lou, dear Lou:
At this moment, now, Saturday, the eleventh of February, at six o'clock, I lay my pen aside after the last completed Elegy, the tenth. The one whose beginning had already been written in Duino (even back then it was meant to come last): "*Someday, at the end of the nightmare of knowing, I may emerge singing praises and jubilation to assenting angels...*" ...only the first twelve lines remain, everything else is new and: yes, very, very glorious!—Think of it! I have been allowed to survive until this. Through everything. Miracle. Grace.—All in a few days. It was a hurricane, as on Duino

95

all that time: all that was fiber in me, tissue, framework, groaned and bent. There was no thought of eating.¹

For 20 years she had been his mentor, his spiritual director, his confessor, his analyst, and his best friend. She had steered him, and called him to purpose, and brought him on. These were her Elegies too.

Ah praise God, *dear* Rainer, how rich his gift to you—and yours to me! I sat and read and cried for joy and it was not just joy at all but something much more powerful, as if a curtain were being parted, rent, and everything were growing quiet and certain and present and good.²

Lou tells him how, "On my way back from Vienna," she has read his translations of some of Michelangelo's poems that he had been working on (but did not publish in his lifetime), "and saw before me how you were climbing after the deepest that has been attained in poetry, and yet it is nothing, even when it comes from this powerful mind—so very, very different from the inexpressibility that has become word through you. And now I think: how he also must have struggled for it; and to you yourself it seemed powerful enough that you would subsume it into your own language. But what is it worth compared to *this* primal text of the soul?"

Rilke had copied out and sent her three of the Elegies: the Sixth, the Eighth, and the Tenth.

Through Rilke's translations, she was previously enabled to apprehend, vicariously, how Michelangelo struggled to express what was on his soul, as an artist. Rilke, now, has gone beyond channeling the artistic struggle of Michelangelo, perhaps the greatest painter of all time when it came to "this primal text of the soul."

The *Duino Elegies*, although nostalgic, say primal words about enchantment—only it is a dark enchantment. The reason is not now—or not simply—the cohabitation of life with death, of life *in* death, which is dark enough in Rilke's poetry; but the Elegies are a signing-off on an age, the Christian era, perhaps, and a glimpse—that lets us glimpse too—of the work ahead, beyond war and its eponymous peace, and beyond the war on the world which we call industrialization and technology, beyond political "isms" with their false solutions, to the inter-faith work of restoring the earth to its angel.

That you are there, dear, dear Lou, to seal it so joyously in my inmost heart with your response! As I read your good, assenting letter: how it flooded me anew, this certainty from all sides that it is *here* now, *here*, this thing that has gestated so long, from the very start.³

Rilke copies out the rest of the Elegies and inserts them in subsequent letters that are now flying back and forth between the pair. Lou writes in one letter:

To feel such a sun-time so utterly is given only to human beings like you: the ones who take risks, the ones who go on and on endangering themselves, for whom at any moment any season could topple over into an absolute light-blind wintriness.⁴

One thinks of Hölderlin, Ruskin, and Nietzsche, who all went insane before the end.

For the creator who will enchant us, enchantment is a *task*. Enchantment is a task in our time, in any time perhaps, although the *resistances* differ between one time and another. Even we who seek enchantment, who realize that there is no soulfulness without enchantment and who realize that soullessness and disenchantment go equally together, even for us soul-work is a task. The resistances to soul-work and enchantment in our time come under the umbrella name of "the economy," which means, now that state socialism is dead, commodity capitalism, its enemy, which is no better. This "economy" is a total system which, as our brain-child, comes back to get even and get inside, to govern our choices, desires, hopes, and wishes. To commodity capitalism, enchantment is a resistance. It is a powerful means because it works on our inner life, within our inner sensitivity and sensibility, with a contrary indication to every totalizing objectivism and realism that capitalism conjugates.

Lou could read the Elegies straight away for she had been party to their creation.

The most powerful and at the same time gentlest [Elegy] for me is the Ninth. There reading, reading on to the end, is scarcely possible, as in gardens whose paths one can't even use as paths, since what is blooming and greening all around slows down every step, brings to a halt; again and again, in every stanza, every section of a stanza, I sit down, feel myself in a bower, as if little branches were plaiting themselves together above me into an unheard-of homeland.[5]

This is reading as soul-work. But I must warn my reader. These Elegies that it took a poet, a master of soul-work as great as Rilke, 10 years to write, we will not read in a day. It must *take time* before we know what Lou means where she writes: "*I can never tell you*: how much this means to me and how I have unconsciously been waiting to receive what is *Yours* as also *Mine*, as life's true consummation."[6]

The pressing into her in order to take form inside her that Rilke wrote in *Narcissus* has, at last, managed to come true. What Rilke has now achieved is the unification of self and nature, of drives of self-preservation and self-sacrifice, of depths and surfaces, *of melancholy and enchantment*.

The melancholy is because we are estranged from the "homeland," as Lou calls it. The homeland can mean different things: paradise that was, heaven that will be; but in any case "we are not at home in this interpreted world," as Rilke says in the First Elegy. In the Narcissus myth, our un-at-home-ness (*unheimlichkeit*) is the self-alienation. My image is me and not-me. And I am *this*, the kind of being that can be both me and not-me *at one and the same time*; and the world is a world in which this is the case; such is this world! Hence, my melancholy.

And the Elegies are about the dead who have gone before us. A melancholy prospect—for we are joining them. Not soon. Already.

In singing the praises of the Angel, Rilke sings praise to our unseen unity with the dead.

This unity is an experience of the soul, which the Elegies speak forth.

The dead are not dead; they are where the young Lament leads us (Tenth Elegy):[7]

> Only those who died young, in their first state
> of timeless equanimity, that of being weaned,
> follow her lovingly. She waits
> for girls and befriends them. She shows them gently
> what she is wearing. Pearls of grief and the fine
> veils of suffering.—With youths she walks on
> in silence.

The young Lament leads out to the valley of Lament. Even human beings, we living, she reminds he who follows, know us, when in their mines or on their mountain ranges they sometimes find "a lump of polished primal grief or the lava of frozen rage from some old volcano." Yes, we living know these well. And she leads him into the wide landscape of Lament and shows him "the columns of old temple...Tear trees and fields of flowering Sadness," where he sees herds of Grief, grazing, and the Lament leads on, out toward the mountains of primal grief.

All this happens behind the façades of our daily living. Only when we can fight free of all the distractions, which distract us from soul and soulfulness, can we follow, as we must.

For the dead are there—only we have our backs turned to them and all our senses turned away from them.

The dead have life. The Angel is witness and testifies:

> Angel: if there were a place we know nothing of, and there,
> on some unsayable carpet, lovers revealed
> what here they could never master, their high daring
> figures of heart's flight,
> their towers of desire, their ladders,
> long since standing where there was no ground, leaning,
> trembling, on each other—and mastered them,
> in front of the circle of watchers, the countless, soundless dead:
> Would these not fling their last, ever-saved,

> ever-hidden, unknown to us, eternally
> valid coins of happiness in front of the finally
> truly smiling pair on the silent
> carpet? (Fifth Elegy)

Yes, it is possible. But, for the animal, it is not like it is for us:

> The creature gazes out into openness with all
> its eyes. But our eyes are
> as if they were reversed, and surround it,
> everywhere, like barriers against its free passage. (Eighth Elegy)

The *open* is where the curtain dividing the living from the dead is rent from top to bottom and, there, one can see through the rent. In the open, there is no "life" and "death." Our eyes have "not that openness/ that is so deep in the animal's vision. Free from death." (Eighth Elegy)

> We never have pure space in front of us,
> not for a single day, such as flowers open
> endlessly into. Always there is world,
> and never the Nowhere without the Not: the pure,
> unwatched over, that one breathes and
> endlessly knows, without craving. (Eighth Elegy)

"Lovers are close to it" (Eighth Elegy), close to the open, which opens out behind the other...but it turns back to world again. The mute calm look of the animal looks through us and our world to the open.

> And yet in the warm waking creature
> is the care and burden of a great sadness. (Eighth Elegy)

It is not the animal but the Angel that is the creature who can witness to us of the open.

The Angel is the proper name of the unison of melancholy and enchantment in the Elegies.

"Every angel is terror."—the Second Elegy begins by repeating. "And yet,/ ah, knowing you, I invoke you, almost deadly/ birds of the soul." The Angels are not unctuous expressions on Rilke's part, or pseudo-religious imagery,[8] let alone real intermediaries of some sort. Rilke's epistolary explanations have done more damage and caused more confusion in relation to understanding the Elegies than anything anyone else has written badly about them. Lou is right; the Angels are "a horizon" of the soul's experience, "an optically unifying illusion."[9] The enchantment of a "dark rapture," which is death "before the heart of the 'stronger presence'."[10]

Rilke's Angel is a word for metaphysical experience. "Experience" is the key word that unlocks the Elegies, just as Rilke said to Lou was the case with *The Notebook of Malte Laurids Brigge*. To read the Elegies, we must learn to read them until the words sound in our soul, just as, for Swann, the words "two or three times" or "I knew what she was after" carved themselves on the living tissues of his heart, else their music must haunt us like Vinteuil's sonata. The Elegies enable us to experience vicariously, through his words, Rilke's experience—the dark enchantment of Rilke's Angel—for his words capture it. His Elegies provide us the opportunity, were we to read them, of metaphysical experience as soul-work, and soul-work as enchantment.

The dark enchantment of the Elegies turns to *jubilation*. The *experience* of the elegiac and the jubilant become one, as life and death are one.

Rilke knew that religion spoke the nihilistic other-worldly language of *spirit*, rather than the poetic and this-worldly language of *soul*. Perhaps, once, religion had been soul-making, in Medieval times, or, Rilke believed, in Russia; but, in the twentieth century, in Europe where he was, religion was soul-destroying. And many millions of souls would literally be obliterated. And it would be no accident—although something of a bizarre paradox—that the world's worst wars were in the established heartland of Christianity; millions of obliterated souls would be Jews. Politics was the obvious reason, but the religious culture with an immemorial anti-Semitism that crossed denominational and national boundaries belonged to the spiritual context. But the religious Christian (not just the cultural Christian—under which heading I would include the atheist), reading Rilke, is forced to put the soul back at the center of personal being and be "simple-souled."[11] Rilke was not spiritual in the "pure" sense that seeks to purge itself of all that is "unclean" and "unholy"; he was soulful, which means *purity is creativity* and psychological depth. As a soul-worker, he knew melancholy, the ground-mood of the soul that opens the soul to the enchantment that is the desire of the soul.

In a letter Rilke writes, "Whoever does not, sometime or other give his full consent, his full *joyous* consent, to the dreadfulness of life, can never take possession of the unutterable abundance and power of our existence; can only walk on its edge, and one day, when the judgment is given, will have been neither alive nor dead. To show the *identity* of dreadfulness and bliss, these two faces on the same divine head, indeed, this one *single* face, which just presents itself this way or that, according to our distance from it or the state of mind in which we perceive it—this it the true significance and purpose of the Elegies and the Sonnets to Orpheus."[12]

To these marvelous serious and joyous Sonnets we now turn.

Notes

1. Rilke and Salomé, *Letters*, 331. (Italics in original)
2. Ibid., 333.
3. Ibid., 334.
4. Ibid., 337.
5. Ibid., 338.
6. Ibid., 338. (Italics in original)
7. All excerpts from the Elegies in this chapter are from the translation by A.S. Kline (2001), <http://www.poetryintranslation.com> (accessed January 2, 2010).
8. This is what Adorno thought in "Theses upon Art and Religion," *Notes to Literature*, Volume 2, 294.
9. Salomé, *You Alone Are Real to Me*, 110.
10. Ibid., 118.
11. Rilke, *Selected Letters*, trans. R.F.C. Hull (Macmillan: London, 1946), 336.
12. Rilke, Letter of April 12, 1923 to Countess Margot Sizzo-Noris-Crouy. *Briefe*, 2 vols. (Wiesbaden: Insel Verlag, 1950), II, 407.

11

"The little rust-colored sail"

In his letter to von Hulewicz, "the little rust-colored sail" of the *Sonnets to Orpheus* is how Rilke compares them to "the gigantic white canvas of the Elegies."[1]

Before we turn to the Sonnets, let us pause. We have entered into Rilke's world now, quite deeply, and hopefully have already begun to be affected by it, or to feel the potential effect that it could have on us, if we *persist in reading*. But what appreciation of enchantment and the work of enchantment has it brought us? I may just comment on this in order to highlight a few points.

First, enchantment is an erotic relationship, and although we may be blasé about reading, listening, and gazing, they too are erotic activities. We need sex in our minds and senses; that is to say, we need that *procreative power* in our minds and in our senses. For it is this procreative power that gives birth to enchantment, or allows our insemination by the seeds of that which is enchanting. Reading, listening, and gazing do this—at least they do so in their proper meaning, which we distinguished at the outset from their mundane meaning.

Secondly, enchantment is narcissistic. It is our response-ability. At the heart of every act of enchantment is self-love and self-surrender, Lou Salomé taught. This translates into saying, for example, "I am reading this for myself"—Rilke's Sonnets, say—but to do so, I must surrender myself. And the same goes for every work of enchantment. If I am gazing at a picture by Vermeer, looking for that little patch of yellow wall, or if I am listening to a work of a well-known composer, I am both doing it absolutely for myself (maybe with others, who, equally, are doing it for themselves) and, by the same act, totally surrendering myself to that picture (with a devotion like Bergotte's) or that piece of music.

So the work of enchantment is erotic and narcissistic, and the two go together. Thirdly, my last point before we get into the Sonnets, we need a turning. We need something, some work of art, or some love of our life—even some Odette perhaps—that will switch our sensibilities the right way, in the right direction and orient us. It is my claim that the works of Proust, Rilke, and Goethe do this, but that is a very narrow claim. There are many arts and, in every one of them, many great artists. Great art is the art that can provide such a turning; mediocre art cannot. And, of course, there is a lot of rubbish which calls itself "art," but does so merely out of vanity or stupidity. But, before, I said it was a sign of great art that it abides; and to that I would add that great art abides because it has this "turning" quality.

Here then, with these recapitulatory comments summing up the last few chapters, we may turn back to Rilke, for whom the kinds of things I am saying are taken for granted. Enchantment for Rilke, as we will see now, is really to develop powerfully our inwardness as sensibility and sensitivity to all creation.

"The Elegies set up this norm of existence," Rilke tells von Hulewicz.[2]

This norm is that we become "transmuters of the earth,"[3] which is to say, we "transform" (*Verwand*, to use Rilke's word) or we might say "transubstantiate" the earth into ourselves, and, we might add, transubstantiate ourselves into the earth (which is our physical destiny in any case). What this means, I think, is that we become the channels between life and death, or, more precisely, between lament and jubilation.

But how do we do this?—*If we become enchanted*, if "our whole existence here, the flights and falls of our love, all strengthen us for this task (beside which there really is no other)."

It starts with reading, listening, and gazing as primary educational activities of the soul. They are educational because they educe, they bring out soul from amidst the walls of the self and its precepts.

The Sonnets, Rilke tells von Hulewicz, "reveal single aspects of this activity."

Elegies and Sonnets sustain each other at all points.

The *Sonnets to Orpheus* are in honor of him, Orpheus. He went into the underworld and rescued Eurydice by guiding the way through the dark with his music.

Rilke's Sonnets are sonnets of praise because he (Rilke) has been, in a sense, Eurydice, and has listened to Orpheus's music in his soul and found his way out to the light. He has written the Elegies as if to say, "See, I've been there!"

The Sonnets are light, jubilant—even, at points, for a serious poet like Rilke, frivolous. He wrote them quickly; for him, in a rush; and he believed in their inspiration, which is why he left them rather than begin to work on them to make some of them better poetry. Those who criticize the Sonnets at the level of poetic technique have not begun to understand what they signify at the level of their enchantment and the world of enchantment: they belong to a post-Elegies world, for they are indicative of a changed inner prospect. It is this which the reader needs to appreciate.

> But still for us existence is enchanted: from a
> hundred places
> it is still origin. A play of pure forces
> that no-one touches unless he kneels and admires. (II.10)[4]

It is not the perfection or imperfection of the Sonnets that matters, but the overflowing (cf. II.22), which of course they represent, but which, more importantly, they transubstantiate into word, so that the word can enter us and enchant us likewise.

The Sonnets are divided into two books—of 26 and 29 Sonnets, respectively. They may be read quickly and re-read, rather than pondered on.

Rilke dedicated the Sonnets to Vera Ouckama Knoop, a beautiful young teenage dancer who died, if we are to believe I.25, from a fatal blood condition, perhaps leukemia, of which Rilke himself was to die, although Rilke never knew the proper name of the disease which afflicted him and took him to his deathbed because he refused anyone in his presence to mention the name. As far as he was concerned, he was dying the death which was *his*, the death to which his life had given birth. He was dying because he was mortal, but the author of the Elegies and the Sonnets had been there and back, and so he knew where he was going; and he was aware young Vera, who he hardly knew, was not far away.

As a dancer, the transformative expressive power of the body was her element:

Dancer: oh you translation
of all transiency into action, how you made it clear! (II.18)

Vera's death is as much sung as lamented:

Sickness drew near. Already by shadows mastered,
the darkened blood, half-suspect, could not wait,
but surged, toward its natural springtime bounding.

Again and again, interrupted by dark and disaster,
it glittered, earthly. Till after terrible pounding
it entered the desolate open gate. (I.25)

But on the very next page, it is affirmed that Orpheus sings in all things:

Finally, driven by vengeance, they broke and tore
your body, but in cliffs and lions lingered
your music, in birds and trees. You still sing there. (I.26)

The song is one breath through life and death. "Breath" is of course *pneuma* in Greek, which, in Latin, is *spiritus*, and, in English, "spirit."

The Sonnets are primarily occupied with this breath, but it is more of a note upon which we hear Orpheus's lyre that Rilke celebrates here. Rilke both identifies with Orpheus and dis-identifies with him. Rilke's "Orphism" is not a new attempt at cult, or a "New Age" spirituality. After 20 centuries of Christianity in Europe, the figure of Orpheus as a god of transformations, including the transformation from life to death, and from death to life, the idea of rebirth, is still alive and well. Rilke's "Orphism" is an *aesthetic* which perhaps belongs in more than one world. It harks back, at least, to a Magian spirit and to pagan myth like a Renaissance painting in an Italian church, but then it would have us see in creation a beauty that is levity and a "song" which vibrates through matter and can make even the stones cry out, but that has been lost to historic Christianity because of its rationalism and moralism. Rilke points beyond this world. And so Orpheus (who stands in the mythical world) does not displace the Angels of the Elegies (of the world to come). They are both of this world and its imagination.

> O you God that has vanished! You infinite track!
> only because dismembering hatred dispersed you
> are we hearers today and a mouth which else nature would lack. (I.26)[5]

The world Rilke wrote in was full of a dismembering hatred which would tear Europe and the world apart. Big ideology would co-opt myth for its own purposes. For instance, what mythic power would the color red hold for millions! Christianity, insofar as it is pagan, turns its history and the sayings of Jesus and his disciples into philosophical metaphysics, the new discourse of theology, and, in the long run, into an architectonic belief system that purports to "know" about God as, for instance, Trinity. The Reformation only hardened this tendency to "truth" as systematic theology, while, at the same time, purporting to rely on "scripture alone." Christianity, insofar as it is Jewish, as Jesus and the disciples all were, is an instructive ethic. Christianity tells us, today, to bring some light into someone's life by doing something for him or her. This is not myth but the spirit of a law and points to a duty. However, Christianity in Rilke's Europe was about to implode, and ours is the time of the aftermath.

But Rilke's poetry, it is my belief, is untimely, for he knew that he, like Lou, Nietzsche, and Freud, and contemporary artists who influenced him—Tolstoy, Rodin, Cézanne, Mallarmé, and Valéry— were all working for a time beyond the one they were mired in; perhaps, for the time of the aftermath; certainly for a future time not their own.

For Christmas 1923, Rilke sent Lou, in Göttingen, special limited editions of the Elegies and the Sonnets. He inscribed the Elegies:

For *Lou*,
who has owned it with me from the first, this now in its ultimate form,
Rainer.

In the Sonnets he inscribed:

Lou

Rainer

(in the spirit of Christmas)

Lou had been in Berlin since the end of September and did not get home until March 1924. She had initially gone to attend the psychoanalytical congress, where she had stayed at Eitingon's Biedermeier, where the Freuds had stayed as well. Eitingon had founded the polyclinic, as it was known, in Berlin, where psychoanalysis was practiced. Lou stayed on, working there. But at last, back at Loufried, her home in Göttingen, she wrote on 16 March to Rilke at Muzot.

> In the middle of the room, as its very centre, your two books, consummated and come home. All the way to the blue of their covers so full of memories.[6]

A picture rather reminiscent of Proust's description of Bergotte's books, "arranged three by three kept watch like angels with outspread wings and seemed for him who was no more, the symbol of his resurrection."

Rilke's work too will raise the dead.

"But I *must* tell you something further immediately," Lou goes on, "namely, the experiences I had using handwritten versions of your poems with damaged, recovering patients. They were the sort of people for whom, as a result of their neurosis, everything had become dead, and they felt no differently about their own lives: they existed in a deep apathy, and it caused anything alive—human, creature, nature—to turn immediately into a thing for them, into a material object, a worthless non-thing, in the end garbage, a cast-off piece of filth. This produces severe states of anxiety, bitter terror: dead among dead things."

"Dead among dead things." This is the perfect expression of soullessness and an indictment of the commodity capitalism that brings it about in us by turning all things into objects of monetary value and potential profit or loss. We remember, in his letter to von Hulewicz, Rilke had said:

> Nature, and the objects of our environment and usage, are but frail, ephemeral things; yet, as long as we are here, they are our possession and our friendship, knowing our wretchedness and our joy, just as they were the familiars of our ancestors. Thus, it is meet for us not only not to pollute and degrade the Actual, but precisely because of the transitoriness which it shares with us, we should seize these things and appearances with the most fervent comprehension and transform them.[7]

"Transform" means, in our language, things must be allowed, and made able, *to enchant us*.

Rilke's idea of "possession" is not capitalist acquisition and ownership—the scourges of our world—the idea that we possess things, though things possess *us*.

"Even for our grandfathers," Rilke goes on to point out to von Hulewicz, "a house, a fountain, a familiar tower, their very clothes, their coat, was infinitely more, infinitely more intimate; almost every object a vessel in which they found something human or added their morsel of humanity."

The intimacy of things is also the intimacy of beauty to truth—truth here being not some delusory metaphysics of speculation but the veracity of *proper names*: coat, fountain, tower, gate, and tree.

But commodity capitalism surreptitiously wars on things and on proper names and destroys both together.

"Now, from America," Rilke continues, "empty, indifferent things crowd over to us, counterfeit things, the veriest dummies. A house, in the American sense, and American apple or one of the vines of that country has *nothing* in common with the house, the fruit, the grape into which have entered the hope and meditation of our forefathers. The lived and living things, the things that share our thoughts, these are on the decline and can no more be replaced. *We are perhaps the last to have known such things.*"

Rilke is not talking about going back to how things were; he is not here expressing some kind of reactionary conservatism, which is how he is most often taken. He is not stupid, he knows that turning the clock back is impossible, and he knows Europe is on the brink of further disaster. He knows that, whatever happens, the world cannot move forward in any shape or form without enchantment. If we lose that we lose ourselves. Our humanity, our humanism, is tied to the health and well-being of enchantment, which in turn is tied to *things*: a coat, a tower, a tree, a piazza, and an old pearl-handled hairbrush.

Little could Rilke see that people would no longer afford to live in houses, but would live in "flats" or "units." And the home would become more and more like a mini-leisure center kitted out with the devices and gimmicks which a capitalist economic system invents to retain our continued subservient loyalty to it. The mockery is that people with these things count themselves *happy*; and poverty is measured by *not* having them. Little could Rilke see wine become totally disconnected from the particularity of place, field, and the fence, from what the French call *terroir* to refer to particular soil, climate, and conditions in a specific year. All this has gone and been replaced with blending grape types in massive industrial vats to obtain "flavor," a ruination of the grape supported by a self-serving industry of "expert" tasters, wine journalists, and "connoisseurs." Little could Rilke have foreseen our genetically modified force-fed fruits (and now animals)—all tasteless—but that look good in the shop, even if, as in the case of bruise-free identical, manufactured apples, the cores may be rotten from radiation. What about the American corporation which "plays God" by purporting to own seed, so that anyone who uses it without paying may be sued and possibly imprisoned? The monopolization which commodity capitalism naturally tends toward—hence its lean toward totalitarianism, not freedom, as is evident from plain experience—sees the kind of company that can "play God" as the ultimate goal, where the whole market is theirs and theirs alone. And such helpless complaints as these are already so familiar to our ears that we have become numb and indifferent to them; even though it is *our* fate at stake. Rilke *could* see the idolatry but not envisage the global "playing out" which we are witnessing today.

Rilke's words, and his poems, point to a world beyond commodity capitalism, and after Capitalist rule; they do not essentially point back to Old Europe, to the world as it ostensibly was before. His words point at what is *in us* as the possibility for enchantment, but what, invisibly, with ghostly power, commodity capitalism sucks out of us.

So often, Rilke's words, quoted above, are criticized as being specious and are quickly dismissed. However, they are a core text that connects with his poetry, as well as everything we are saying in this book about enchantment. Only with Rilke's words in mind can we see how difficult or well-nigh impossible enchantment is in our world, and how easy it is to become "*dead among dead things.*"

Lou knew Rilke's mind on this better than anyone ever did. But let us pick up her letter to him where we left off:

> Different moments can bring about the resolution in a recovering patient: on a forest trail above our house, a woman with agoraphobia first saw trees *lived* and what the harvested fields expressed so clearly and with such yellowness and she cried out in delight over the force and strength of the world that had suddenly been given back to her and was accepting into herself her liberated steps. But there were others who sat up and took notice for the first time

when they heard *your* tone as that of Life: and it was indescribably moving that they heard and understood *it* before they were capable of grasping even the most readily understandable attributes of the day around them, much less any experience from the realm of art, *as something alive*. And not one of them had previously had some special relationship to poetry, rather the opposite: what resounded there had come all the way across to them only because those who have been blessed as artists and those who have been stripped of their blessings by an affliction live in a single region, in close proximity and at the same depth—for Heaven and Hell are not at all *two* places.

They are two ways of being in the same place and in this world. In his earliest poetry, which Rilke "placed into the hands of Lou" in his dedication to the *Book of Hours* (1905), Rilke saw people in hell in our cities—especially those crushed by capitalist poverty, which is so different from the holy poverty and which Rilke celebrates as heavenly and free. The other way is this way that Lou discovered upon reading.

Lou found Rilke's Elegies and Sonnets revived people and *brought them back from the dead*.

Suddenly, these patients became enchanted with the world. Sometimes we have to be patients first, before this becomes a possibility. Otherwise we can continue in our capitalist consumer-induced miasma, working for leisure and eponymous happiness, for which the economic system defines the terms.

Upon receipt of this letter, Rilke wrote back[8]; his first line confirms what we have been saying:

My dear dear Lou,

I cannot tell you what a grand, marvelous *Easter* you have brought me with your letter...

Notes

1. Rilke, *Selected Letters*, 396.
2. Ibid., 395.
3. Ibid., 396.
4. Rilke, *Sonnets to Orpheus*, trans. C.F. MacIntyre (Berkeley/Los Angeles: University of California, 1960), 75.
5. Rilke, *Later Poems*, trans. J.B. Leishman (London: Hogarth Press, 1938), 170.
6. Rilke and Salomé, *Letters*, 345.
7. Rilke, *Selected Letters*, 394.
8. Rilke and Salomé, *Letters*, 347.

12

The Frame of Enchantment

Goethe's Wilhelm Meister novels are a primary text of the work of enchantment.

We turn to them last of all. While Adorno, who we encountered at the start of this book, helped provide some conceptual coordinates with respect to the importance of enchantment and the historical "moment" of it, now, with Goethe, we find a theoretician of enchantment itself—or one who was virtually so. We will see here and in the next chapter how enchantment compasses us about.

In something that is enchanting, our inner sensibility for it, our sensitive capacity for it, comes together with that thing. It might be a thing literally, as in Rilke, who valued craftwork and loved objects, such as dolls, or it might be a person; but, whatever the case, that person or that thing come together in a *time* of enchantment.

Ultimately, *enchantment is a quality of time*. From childhood, we are predisposed to enchantment; but it is only as adults that the really *erotic* quality of enchantment and the *work* of enchantment may be fully formed. And then it is the work of a lifetime—this reading, this listening, this gazing. It is principally what we should work at to give our time to. If we have time, it is what we should have time for, because, if we give it time, later we would not come to look back and regret lost time but, rather, we will come to have found eternity in time, which is to die in peace.

We need to develop, that is, enrich and deepen, our soul, the unison of our inner sensibility and sensitivity, for a time of enchantment; and this is precisely what the work of enchantment does: it leads to that enrichment, it *is* that enrichment. Reading, listening, and gazing, far from being time-filling activities, are what, more than ever in a workaday world governed by consumerist greed and nonchalance, are required for health and flourishing, and you cannot buy them. All you can do is *give them time*.

So we move sideways again—this time, from Rilke to Goethe—to stand in front of yet another icon, through which the lineaments of our subject of enchantment and the concomitant *work* of enchantment look different again. However, to appreciate this, as with Proust and Rilke, in my comments here on Goethe I presuppose no prior knowledge of his work. My comments then will have the secondary advantage of providing some introduction to it.

Enchantment can never be fixed; we see it differently through different apertures. To demonstrate this, the present chapter and the one to follow will be longer than previous ones because, this time, we are interested in the narrative whole, which was not the case with Proust or Rilke. Also, I need to intersperse my comments with my description of the narrative as we go. But at the end of each chapter I will repeat in summary form, as I have on other occasions, what is to be learned by entering into the deep worlds of enchantment supplied by our chosen icon—in this case, Goethe's mature writings.

The Wilhelm Meister novels are not merely a series or a cycle, but a unity, although it is arguable which particular texts comprise that unity.[1]

In this chapter I will only say a brief word about *Wilhelm Meister's Apprenticeship* because I want to focus on enchantment in a way that extends our discussion, and *Wilhelm Meister's Journeyman Years* will do this more richly.

However, as background information, let us note that *Wilhelm Meister's Apprenticeship* shows the young Wilhelm turns away from the life of the bourgeois, and, to some extent, from bourgeois capitalism, to the way of the artist and the outsider—in this case, the life of the wandering theater troupe. The theater troupe still depends on financial patronage from the system and so is not, of course, completely outside the economy, but, as Wilhelm's businessman brother constantly reminds him—"come back"—, he is in danger. He is sufficiently an outsider to be in danger of homelessness, complete penury and, indeed, of losing his life. As it is though, mostly thanks to Wilhelm, the theater troupe is successful, and he meets "salt of the earth" types; and he ends up engaged to marry the woman of his dreams, the beautiful Natalie.

In the background of the story told in the *Apprenticeship* are the rumblings not just of civil strife, but of changing times. The theater troupe is committed to change: different towns, different plays, different relationships; changing roles and costumes on and off stage. The world they pass through is ostensibly stable—only it is not. And this, the reader can note, is like the instability of our own times and societies. At the simplest level: every act has consequences, foreseen and unforeseen; multiply this by the population and by the number of social acts in a day and already you have a colossal number of sequelae, and a presentiment that life, even in stable centers of commerce, is on the move and changing. Leaders may endeavor to keep a lid on change and preserve stability but any modern understanding of subjectivity tells us that this is not how the world turns, or how values operate. Impermanence is of the essence; in this sense, the actor's precarious existence is closer to the truth, or, at least, a reminder of it. As Shakespeare declared, "All the world's a stage/ And all the men and women merely players."[2]

The success of Wilhelm's troupe is not brought about by pandering to the "lowest common denominator," as we might be accustomed to today, in order to attract the advertising dollar. Wilhelm introduces *Hamlet* in a central part of the novel and there is detailed discussion of the importance of Shakespeare's work and of *Hamlet* in particular.[3] There is a sense, then, that these outsiders, this little acting troupe, on the edge of a world on the boil, are carrying inestimable goods: the transmission of true culture as instanced by Shakespeare's *Hamlet*. The true center of the world, therefore, we are led to think in the novel, is not the "business district" of town or the "banking sector" of the economy, but here among this motley crew at the margins of decent society. This is to remain the "bohemian" and avant-garde ideal for European artists for the next 200 years. And *Hamlet* as a work of art outsmarts all attempts to "encapsulate" it once and for all, to "appropriate" it, as we say in postmodern jargon. It is a true work of art that continues to speak, and to speak of humankind's wisdom and folly. Moreover, it is in just such a work of art, through time and across place, that we continue to see ourselves reflected. This is the only way we can see ourselves: by just such a gaze into just such a mirror. *Hamlet* is one such mirror, the *Journeyman Years* another, and *Faust* yet another.

In the *Conversations of German Refugees*, a fragment related to the Wilhelm Meister cycle, the Germans are fleeing the French. It is the aftermath of the French Revolution, presumably "when the Frankish army burst into our land through a breach in our defenses." The Baroness, one of the interlocutors, says what people might have said in Germany under National Socialism—and surely did: "I don't know what has got into us, how all civilized behavior can so suddenly disappear."[4] Well how does it disappear? Goethe's answer—and the Conversations are demonstrative in this regard—is that the loss of good manners, of simply being polite, augurs worse things to come. While, as André Comte-Sponville says, a polite Nazi is still a Nazi, but if you take it that there are no natural virtues, so that we must *become* virtuous, then morality must start somewhere. Politeness is a formal quality that is supposed to pave the way for virtue.[5]

Good conversation is impossible, virtue is impossible, diplomacy is impossible, without the pre-condition which consists in civilized, good manners, which underscores the importance of social ritual. The assault on manners in contemporary society, Goethe would think, is not what it seems, that is, harm-free; and it certainly is not "progressive" in any sense at all.

War starts within us. "At the present time among a huge mass of unfortunates hardly anyone, whether through temperament or education, by accident or by effort of will, enjoys peace of mind," the Baroness says to her little band.[6] This is what comes to the surface first when good manners are removed. At the same time, there is a turn to "the news." Hence, from these conversations all mention of the news is forbidden. Later we learn why. "What makes news attractive? Not its importance, not its consequences, but its novelty. For the most part only what is new seems important, because it is without clear context, it arouses amazement, momentarily stirs our imagination, just grazes our emotions, and requires no mental effort whatever. Everyone can take a lively interest in such new things without the least trouble to themselves. Indeed, since a series of news items continually pulls us from one subject to the next, most people find nothing more pleasant than this stimulus to ceaseless diversion, this convenient and never-ending opportunity to vent their malice and spleen."[7]

Goethe puts what we may take to be his own wisdom into the mouth of his interlocutor. The more that *manners* abate, the more news interferes in every area of our life. Translate this to today. In our society, thanks to the communications industry, the news industry can trawl the web for the most titillating stories of horror and disaster and line them up back-to-back to present as "World News." The refugees in Goethe's story refuse (this is their renunciation) to talk about the news. They talk about all manner of other things, eventually settling on storytelling as the most worthwhile form of conversation and, in particular, stories about the way that our inner sensibility and sensitivity can affect our physical health, and love in particular: we have all heard of love-sickness; we have all been in love. And so stories of love have a very personal bearing for each of the speakers.

The attack on "the news" (which both Schopenhauer and Hegel were later to disparage) continues in the section of aphorisms in the *Journeyman Years*. "To my mind, the greatest evil of our time, which allows nothing to come to fruition, is that each moment consumes its predecessor, each day is squandered in the next, and so we live perpetually from hand to mouth, without ever producing anything. Do we not already have newspapers for each part of the day! Some clever soul could probably insert one or two more. The result is that everyone's deeds, actions, scribblings, indeed all his intentions are dragged before the public. No-one is permitted to rejoice or sorrow except to entertain all the rest; and so everything leaps from house to house, from town to town, from empire to empire, and finally from continent to continent, always express."[8]

Reiterating this same point in postmodernism, Michel de Certeau describes the mind-forged manacles that pass for the news as follows:

"Narrations about what's-going-on constitute our orthodoxy. Debates about figures are our theological wars. The combatants no longer bear the arms of any offensive or defensive idea. They move forward camouflaged as facts, data, and events. They present themselves as messengers from a 'reality'. Their uniform takes on the color of the economic and social ground they move into. When they advance, the terrain itself seems to advance. But in fact they fabricate the terrain, simulate it, use it as a mask, accredit themselves by it, and thus create the scene of their law."[9]

Why this attack on the news is important with regard to enchantment will become clearer as we proceed, but we can say straight away that it is because "news" in this sense *commodifies time* and commodifies moments of time. In a news and instant communications environment, *enchantment is impossible*. Goethe foresees this in the eighteenth century, not because he had "second sight" or anything like that, but simply because it logically follows from what he could already see going on in his day. News, current affairs, celebrity gossip, and the like come to comprise a lifestyle of idle reading, listening, and gazing so, instead of being conduits to enchantment, which they should be, they become means of consumption.

Another interesting topic which can be traced in the *Journeyman Years* is the difference between men and women. *The essence of woman is to be enchanting*; this is within woman's power, and not man's. We will take this up later. On men, the Baroness comments how, although for there to be society there must be manners, and therefore people must practice self-control as a basic precondition for manners, the culprits are not women, but men. "How easily men can deceive themselves especially where self-control is concerned!"[10] It is men who make wars, not women; but women and children—those who are most enchanting of all—are the major sufferers from war. "I have never in my life met one single man who was capable of controlling himself in even the smallest detail."[11] The current tendency of western society is to mingle or confuse male and female: the masculinized woman of the "workplace" who is the same as a man—or should be, or the domesticated woman "at home" who is supposedly pitiable by contrast; the man in touch with his feminine side, or the "alpha male" in denial of it. Between these four, femaleness as enchanting is lost, and the woman as enchantress becomes an impossibility. There can be no enchantment in a society where the women are not enchanting and where the men are either too "wet" or too "hard" to be enchanted. But Goethe paints a different picture for a world almost deafened and blinded by war, and its subtle preconditions of the soul, in which all of us are refugees.

Goethe's German refugees are the first "wanderers" and "renunciants"; they wander through "the enchanting countryside"[12]—all themes which will play out in *Journeyman Years*. The first thing to say about *Journeyman Years* is that it is technically complicated, even by more modern literary standards. The novel masters and integrates instances from a huge range of genres: narrative, flashbacks, story-within-the-story, diary, letters, drama, fairytale, address, poetry, a drawing, aphorisms, an "interpolation" or narrative break right in the middle[13]; and the book ends before the end just as it begins before the beginning. The whole story is told through all these means to form a whole which is not sealed in and can never be final, but only always open to interpretation.[14]

At the start of the *Journeyman Years*, Wilhelm is on his way from Natalie, his love; he has delayed their marriage. This is the first renunciation: Wilhelm's personal consummation is put at the disposal of a greater collective consumption, although he is not exactly sure (and neither is the reader) what this is. At the end of the novel, a group of émigrés led by Lenardo are setting out for America, as for a Promised Land. These émigrés at the end are a counterpart of, on the one hand, the refugees in the story, present from before the novel's beginning, and, on the other, Wilhelm's renunciation of making a life and home with Natalie, at the beginning of the novel. In between, all is movement, process, unpredictability. Just like life really. Wilhelm, we learn, is part of a mysterious brotherhood who later become the émigrés and meantime vow not to remain in one place more than 3 days. This way Wilhelm is forced to keep on the move and to renounce whatever bounty one place or one day has to offer.[15] This is the key renunciation of the title. The renunciation of the moment is the negative side of the striving for the next moment which binds Faust in Goethe's work of that name and which Goethe was writing at the same time.

The spirit of a time is the result of the collective renunciation and striving. If we look at our world we can ascertain the spirit of our collective renunciation and striving because the world is the objectification of it. Civilization strives for peace and harmony; but there is a contradiction because peace and harmony seem to spell stasis, permanence, no further development, our collective self-totalization, and the end of history. Renunciation and striving, however, keep changing things and stay dynamic.

The start of the *Journeyman Years* is bold to the point of fanciful in drawing the reader into an enchanted world. Wilhelm meets Joseph and Mary—she is with child—riding on a donkey in idyllic mountains. It might be imagined that Goethe is painting an idyll for us or romanticizing like a second-rate novelist. As it turns out, in their naming there has been a sense of ironic self-consciousness, even a sense of fun and humor, along with a conventional explanation. The feigned allegory vanishes behind an emergent realism as the characters take on identity for the reader.

Every reader will no doubt have their own favorite set pieces which are to them the most enchanting. One of mine is the young lovers Flavio and Hilarie ice-skating on the frozen lake. This story starts romantically, turns ironic, humorous, and then melodramatic, when Flavio's father interferes. Flavio's father is under a double misapprehension. He wrongly believes Flavio does not love Hilarie, but another girl, and he wrongly believes that Hilarie, who is an adolescent, is actually in love with him. Well, Flavio's father is quickly shorn of his illusions, and it is all written with such a graceful, light touch by Goethe that, for a moment, a reader might well have felt it was they who were skating by moonlight on ice. The enchantment here, as in many other places, leaves us with a sense of festive wellbeing, for a moment.[16]

Not only is the countryside enchanting, and the people, so are buildings and *things*. The whole novel has characters speak and relate to things in the way Rilke would have us do. As Joseph says to Wilhelm in their first conversation: "For if the inanimate is full of life, it can bring forth something alive."[17] Wilhelm adds, "...even from amidst these ruins." The past itself is brought back to life. There is an emphasis throughout on the animate properties of stone.

There is a sense that things, down to every rock, are consecrated. As it says in the Gospel, rocks and stones have so much "within" them that is hidden from us; according to the story of the temptation of Jesus in the wilderness, from stones God could even raise up children of Abraham. For Goethe, this has not to do with the "paradoxical" or "magical" power of God to draw the most animate of creatures from the most inanimate of dead objects, but has to do with the potential of stone and that, in the scheme of things, even the "people of God" should not deem themselves superior to a stone. The geologist named Montan is enchanted by stone. Where in the *Journeyman Years* the characters visit old monasteries or villages, or pubs or way stations, and chateaux, the stone, and the human seem to co-inhabit a place. All this is done with *enchanted realism*, which is a heightened realism that we also find more or less accomplished in the nineteenth-century novel.

Goethe puts none of this enchantment down to Nature herself. He is not naïvely "natural" about nature, like some later writers; he does not depict a "state of nature" prior to culture. The point in Goethe is that the enchanted countryside is *cultivated*; even where there are deep mountains we find order and beauty, which is never just of nature *per se*. In fact, what is moving the émigrés away is the sense that it is all so cultivated there is not "room to move," and America, the utopia they envisage moving to, is the only uncultivated pure wilderness, although we learn that others have arrived there well before our émigrés and begun cultivation.

Wilhelm wanders through an ordered world. Culture means ordering aright (fittingly), listening, and gazing in and at the world so as to establish things as they should be. Culture is like a vehicle that is stable while moving. It becomes more ordered, and the order becomes more detailed or sophisticated; there is almost a Mandarin quality about Goethe's philosophy.

The beautiful woman, whether younger or older, is the central figure of enchantment here. This is not an idealized beauty that can be represented; it is intensely individualized and representable only by the proper name of the woman: Natalie, Hilarie, Makarie, and so on.

If philosophy is the wisdom of love, love is desiring, it is erotic—by which I mean, in the broadest sense, *relational*. Erotic desire is central to the plot and the movement of the novel. It is the particularity of desire that counts and of which the novel tells. And yet, like Narcissus, we find ourselves looking into a mirror in which we are surprised to see ourselves. Or perhaps it might be like looking in a glass darkly, if we do not recognize ourselves. Goethe shows us a purified desire, which is not virginal or sexless, but *reverent*. Reverent desire strives and renounces. Reverent desire radiates out from the enchantress to all things—so it seems, at least, to the man.

Wilhelm sends Felix for education at a Pedagogic Province, which is a highly organized, managed, and socialized environment, although not totalitarian, as reverence *interrupts* the possibility of closure necessary to "the system." In the school where Felix will remain for most of the rest of the novel, a threefold reverence is taught: to God above, as manifested in parents, teachers, and superiors; to the earth beneath, from which we are nourished and also suffer; and thirdly for the neighbor and friends.[18] Religions are judged according to their capacity for reverence, and are to be rated and ranked accordingly. The humanistic secular society depicted is "post-religious" in the confessing sense and can tolerate any religion that validates reverence, which it may do at one of three levels, as one of the three Principals explains to Wilhelm.

But one of the Principals goes on to explain: "From the three reverences springs the highest reverence, reverence for oneself, and the others are born once again from this latter, so that the individual can arrive at the highest attainment of which he or she is capable, so that he or she may view themselves as the finest thing that God and Nature have produced, yes, so that he or she can remain at this height, without being dragged back down again to a common level by presumptuousness and self-centeredness."[19]

Wilhelm responds that this all sounds like commonsense to him. "This profession of faith is already articulated by a great portion of the world, albeit unknowingly," he says.

What is being expressed is simply a sense of common humanity. Yet, the point is that this has to be learnt, and that, once learnt, it may be lost. Also, once the sense of common humanity is learnt, or "naturally" known as the result of being born into a culture which allows these reverences, it has to be re-learnt, so that the three reverences "are born once again" from the point of view of a sense of subjective self. What this suggests is that culture comes *before* nature as far as we human beings are concerned, and what we call "nature" is not simply and straightforwardly "natural," but is a product of culture. Culture gives us to see *this* or *that*, which we now assume to be natural, as nature, and understand it as natural. It sounds counterintuitive, but I am saying that nature is not something *in and of itself*, nor is it natural. Both are rooted in our culture and therefore our history; for culture is a creature of time.

But more closely examined, man is not the measure of all things, as in classical humanism or in the philosophy of Protagoras, as explained by Plato in the dialogue of that name; rather, the terms "God," "world," and "humankind" (or simply "man") have to be understood apart from one another and only in *relation* to one another—that is, if they *can* be understood, which, in the case of the first of these terms, however, is impossible. Otherwise, if we try to understand God in terms of the world or in terms of man, or if we try to understand ourselves in terms of the world and the measurements we make there, we set off on the wrong foot and will never arrive at the destination of understanding that we set out to reach. Enchantment arises from the "rub" due to the "gap" between "God," "world," and "humankind." This "friction" and "spacing" between the three co-ordinates may also be described as a knotting; as they are always somehow knotted; and we are caught in such knots, as it is our culture that makes them; and it is this that Goethe primarily draws our attention to, using enchantment as a primary value by which to tell one kind of knot from another: old tangled knots from new ones only now being made.

The three reverences—to God, world, and humankind—are three, not one, because they are *fundamentally different* reverences; they have dues that need to be paid differently. Only then can the fourth reverence come into play—that soulfulness, being the inward and upward dynamic of being—and the possibility therefore of enchantment.

This frame for enchantment is not a motif within the work, but what, in manifold ways, the *Journeyman Years*, the work itself, is expressive of—if we look at it philosophically and from a distance as a work of art.

The experience of enchantment happens within this frame of reverence. And the experience of enchantment happens in the moment. The book is a veritable catalog (if we look at it unimaginatively for a moment) of enchanted moments. And, of course, the reader can draw the conclusion for herself. These moments are not just that of a book, but of a life. This book wakes us up to that life. We find these successive moments of enchantment not just in good books, but in life. There—in books or life—enchantment is "immortalized" in people or places; for instance, the disused monastery where Joseph based his carpentry business, or the beautiful gardens, orchards, fields, and little lakes, the "natural world" which has been domesticated by cultivation over time, and where, now, men, women, and children can feel "at home."

At the heightened moment of enchantment, say of love, it may be rapturous. Enraptured, we go beyond the enchantment of, say (for a man), the woman of our dreams, toward a realm of the soul nearer obsession, to a dark enchantment, with God or the world. And then, God, world, and humankind seem to coalesce. This is an illusion of enchantment. An example from the *Journeyman Years* of what I mean here is the sexual experience of Wilhelm's youth, which he recalls and describes in a letter to Natalie.

> The older of the boys, however, only a little ahead of me in age, the son of a fisherman, did not seem to enjoy this fooling with the flowers. He was a boy to whom I had been especially drawn as soon as he appeared, and he now invited me to go with him down to the river, which, already of considerable width, flowed not far off. We settled down with fishing rods in a shady spot where scores of little fish darted back and forth in the deep, still, clear water. He kindly showed me what to do, how to bait my line, and I succeeded a few times running in jerking the smallest of these delicate creatures against their will up into the air. As we sat there calmly, leaning against each other, he seemed to grow bored, and called my attention to a sandy spit that stretched out into the water on our side. It would make an excellent bathing

place. He could not resist the temptation, he exclaimed, leaping to his feet, and before I knew it was down below, undressed, and in the water."[20]

Wilhelm continues: "A very strange mood came over me. Grasshoppers danced around me, ants scurried about, colorful beetles hung in the branches, and gold-glittering dragonflies, for so he had called them, hovered and fluttered, phantom-like, at my feet, just as the boy, pulling a large crab from a tangle of roots, held it up gaily for me to see, then skillfully concealed it again in its old place, ready for the catch. It was so hot and sultry all around that one longed to be out of the sun and in the shade, then out of the cool of the shade and down into the cooler water. So it was easy for him to lure me down. He did not have to repeat his invitation often, for I found it irresistible and felt, despite some fear of my parents, as well as wariness toward the unknown element, extraordinary excitement. But once I undressed on the sand, I cautiously ventured into the water, though no farther than the gently sloping bottom permitted. He might let me linger there, moved away in the buoyant element, then swam back, and as he climbed out and stood up to dry off in the light of the sun, I thought my eyes were dazzled by a triple sun: so beautiful was the human form, of which I had never had any notion. He seemed to look at me with the same attention. Quickly dressed, we still faced each other without veils. Our hearts were drawn to one another, and with fiery kisses we swore eternal friendship."

From this passage the sense of an enchanted world and the experience of enraptured enchantment are palpable. These "fiery kisses" are not metaphorical, they are mouth to mouth. But his "eternal friendship" is doomed not to last the day. His friend drowns later that same day with five others in a swimming accident where, trying to save younger children from the strong current, they dragged him under with them in their panic and they all got carried away.

The passion of love is a danger for enchantment, as it leads towards rapture and the collapse of the three distinct reverences into one obsessive or fundamental reverence. Perhaps this is why Christian love is not *eros* but *agape*. *Agape* is dispassionate but relational.

While love is the fabric of enchantment, Goethe's novel shows that passionate loves tend to be lost, such as that just described, or, more elaborately, that between Flavio and Makarie, or between Flavio's father and Hilarie, Flavio's intended. However, events conspire (and, in an enchanted world, with enchanted people, events do conspire) to bring Flavio and Hilarie happily together. On the other hand, the basis for Wilhelm's love for his intended, the beautiful Natalie, gradually wanes, to be replaced by his love for Hersilie, although why this is so we are not told. A bit like Proust's novel, the *Journeyman Years* has different perspectives within it, but no overarching explanation (no total theory) under which it all may fit. Wilhelm himself, as the main character, seems to be replaced by Lenardo halfway through *Journeyman Years*, and it is not made clear to the reader whether Wilhelm will join the émigrés in the end or stay behind. In this, the book mirrors life, where we too are left with a whole clutch of things that ultimately are incomplete, as if life is composed of fragments of love.

What we have, then, in the Wilhelm Meister novels is a work of art to frame all possible theories of enchantment and also, in Goethe's wisdom, to guide us. True love, we may extrapolate, is not true if it is not enchanting and it is only enchanting if it is framed by the three reverences: to God above, the earth beneath our feet, and to those around us. And these reverences are not merely attitudes. We recall from the novel that Wilhelm discovers them only by asking about the physical postures of the boys he saw in the Pedagogic Province. This is significant because it means the reverence must be *embodied*, or it is not reverence. In other words, it is essentially an action, not an attitude. As such, it requires learning and self-mastery.

But is true love possible on this earth even for enchanted souls? Goethe, in the *Journeyman Years*, would appear to raise this question. And another question: how true is true love without true society in which it can, as it were, be as much part of the landscape as the "holy family" were at the beginning of the novel? A society is not true if it is out of step with God above, or the earth beneath; these things too need to rise up invisibly within us even as they gain visibility in our actions. We see the earth in our actions, in the *Journeyman Years*, from the dedication so many of the characters have to craft, and hence the elevation of craft alongside art; both are reverential in the sense we have been speaking about here. God, of course, rises up invisibly within us but becomes visible in our actions in the light that our deeds bring into the lives of others. The God of Love in *Journeyman Years* is a practical postulate, not a metaphysical being.

The *Journeyman Years* is like a frameless mirror mirroring enchantment, and where enchantment is not mirrored it is simply out of the frame. In one of the stories within the story, entitled "Who Is the Traitor?" Lucidor is in love with Lucinde. They are enchanting characters in an enchanted setting. Enchantment puts power into *eros* and moves it toward the real presence of its desire. Lucidor is totally captivated by Lucinde. But the whole world seems to conspire in the wisdom of love. "A country setting has considerable advantage for sociability, particularly when the hosts are thoughtful, sensitive individuals, who have been impelled over the years to come to the aid of the natural potential of their surroundings. Such had been done here."[21] A vivid and fresh description of the surrounds is given, then:

> Adjacent to the residence and the utility buildings lay pleasure gardens, orchards, and mowings; thence one wandered unexpectedly into a wood, through which a lane broad enough for driving wound back and forth. At its centre, at the highest elevation, had been constructed a hall with adjoining chambers. Entering by the main door, one saw in a great mirror the finest view the entire region had to offer, then quickly turned around to recover with the help of reality from the unexpected tableau. For the approach was artfully designed and everything ingeniously hidden to achieve this surprise effect. No one entered without turning with pleasure back and forth from the mirror to Nature and from Nature to the mirror.

This is a description from the novel *of the novel* and the way it mirrors the world. But there is a discrepancy, or an illusion, for we do not find the world in the mirror any more than we can find such a mirror in the world—except for Goethe's work in this instance. And so the mirror operates as an inverted symbol; Goethe has it hold an image in its reflection that does not reflect the world, but may enchant us, but may call reverence forth from us. Although the mirror is pictured in the novel, the novel itself is the mirror. Perhaps we may learn the three reverences—and the fourth, soulfulness—by reading, listening, and gazing. What other way of soulfulness is there? In any case, it is by something like this "mirroring" that the novel frames enchantment. And it is a metaphysical experience to which reading gives access.

And so to return to our story briefly, "Who Is the Traitor?" It is about lovers at cross-purposes, each of whom is mistaken about the heart of each of the others. But when, at last, Lucidor holds Lucinde, his true love, in his arms, they are in the room just described, in front of the mirror. In this image, following our interpretation of the novel as framing enchantment, both Nature and the mirror share the same testimony to true love in the center of the whole landscape, real and mirrored. In this love the three reverences are realized in their actual created beauty; they come together, God, Nature, and the lovers lost to love, and that embrace is itself embraced by all the world and presumably, God himself.

Finally, I will recapitulate the main points of the discussion in this long and involved narrative, with its off-cuts and caesurae. My description has been all too brief, I know, but we may see quite clearly, I think, from what I have said, that enchantment occurs in the cultural knotting of God, world, and humankind. Goethe tries to show us the conditions of a different knotting, if we can see ourselves in his work; and if we can measure ourselves by what he mirrors that is of quite another order. Goethe points to a new style of reverence within science and within religion, which does not tie science to objectivism, which only cuts subject from object, and does not tie religion to metaphysical knowledge, which is only false abstraction, beyond the intuitions of experience.

A new culture is conditional for Goethe upon renunciation and striving, in which we must include our reading, listening, and gazing in the sense I have given them. Goethe's literary work perhaps illustrates better than anything ever written, the hope of a world in which enchantment is a living part of life, a world within a world in which to be reasonable is not an impossibility, and a world no less of renunciation and striving. He portrays the possibility, despite the vicissitudes of war and strife, of a culture of enchantment which is neither idyllic nor idealistic and thus a pastiche. Goethe envisages renunciation and striving of this kind to create an artistic, scientific, and religious culture which is western—with Christian and pagan presuppositions and foundations—but which is an alternative to a culture led by self-interest, the happiness of the masses, authoritarian or evangelical religion, pragmatism, historicism or utilitarianism—in short, the mirrors in which we are framed and caught today. Goethe gives us an *enchanted hope* which is different from, on the one hand, the hope of *ethical humanism*, in which Christianity and secularism collude these days, and from, on the other hand, the hope of *ideological humanism*, which we see on both left and right in politics. Goethe's alternative is a *futuristic humanism* based on enchanted hope, but one based practically on solid education in the arts and sciences. Goethe gives us a vision of another world as the potential of our world.

The ideas arising from the Wilhelm Meister novels that I have recapitulated here may now be complemented by a reading of Goethe's *Faust*. Goethe was writing and rewriting *Faust* at the same time as he was writing the Wilhelm Meister novels—at the end of the eighteenth and the start of the nineteenth centuries. In turning to *Faust* in the next chapter, we will work through it in a similar way to here, that is, by following the narrative flow. This will serve again as an introduction to what is otherwise one of the most complex literary texts in the canon of world literature.

Notes

1. Here, by Goethe's "Wilhelm Meister novels," I mean: *Wilhelm Meister's Apprenticeship* (1796); *Conversations of German Refugees* (1795); *The Fairy Tale* (1795); *Wilhelm Meister's Journeyman Years or The Renunciants* (1821), including both sets of aphorisms, and the poems *Vermächtnis* ("Legacy"), after the first set of aphorisms at the end of Book Two, and *Im ernsten Beinhaus* ("In the Charnel House") added in 1829 after the second set of aphorisms at the end of Book Three. As a bibliophile, where more is better, I have a "maximalist" view of the Wilhelm Meister corpus. A minimalist view would include only the *Apprenticeship* and *Journeyman Years*, without the aphorisms and two poems. However, my comments hold whichever view one takes. The maximalist view is Goethe's own, according to the edition of his collected works that he compiled in preparation for his death.
2. William Shakespeare, *As You Like It*, Act II, Scene VII.

3. As an aside, Shakespeare was a little-regarded playwright in England in Goethe's day, but it was in fact Goethe who was most significant in bringing about Shakespeare's recognition in England and, indeed, across the world.
4. Goethe, *Journeyman Years*, 23.
5. André Comte-Sponville, *A Short Treatise on the Great Virtues*, trans. Catherine Temerson (New York: Vintage, 2003), 7-15.
6. Goethe, *Journeyman Years*, 24f.
7. Goethe, *Journeyman Years*, 25-26.
8. Ibid., 298.
9. Michel de Certeau, *The Practice of Everyday Life*, trans. Steven Rendall (Berkeley/Los Angeles: University of California, 1988), 185-6.
10. Ibid., 22.
11. Ibid.
12. Ibid., 18.
13. Ibid., 266.
14. But the matter is more complicated still. Through most of these genres the novel is playing with: parody, rewriting (both others' work as well as Goethe's own), and burlesque. Sometimes these *ironic* modes of writing are sympathetic to their sources, even Oliver Goldsmith and Laurence Sterne, authors, respectively, of *The Vicar of Wakefield* and *Tristram Shandy*, novels Goethe admired. At other times, Goethe ridicules his sources, usually by bettering them. A specialist reader of *Journeyman Years* will find traces of homage to Homer, Aeschylus, Euripides, Cervantes, Dante, Shakespeare, and Calderon, as well as to less-known contemporaries of Goethe.

    An aphorism from the first group, entitled "Reflections on the Spirit of Wanderers," reads: "Aptness, effectiveness and grace reside not in language itself but in the spirit embodied in it. Thus, it is not left to the individual to confer these desirable qualities on his calculations, speeches, or poems. It is a question of whether Nature has endowed him with the requisite spiritual and moral qualities. Spiritual: the gift of sight and insight; moral: that he may fend off the evil demons that could prevent him from paying honour to the truth." These words seem to apply well to Goethe himself, it seems to me: in the novel, despite the diversity of perspectives it holds (though we can only guess the number of them) and the porous quality of the text (so that the different genres bleed into one another, even while they stand distinct; and so that the history of world literature is allowed into the text from outside, as it were), the hand of a single artist prevails. We always feel we are reading Goethe. Part of the reason for this is enchantment; a spirit of enchantment illuminates the multiplicity, as if from within.

    Upon reading the aphorism just quoted, we, like Pontius Pilate, might ask: "What is truth?" Truth is not scientific correspondence with reality, although science and scientific truth is everywhere evident in the text with regard to the enchanted awe by which various characters are held in thrall by Nature. Another aphorism from the same group tells us: "Truth is constructive." Truth is what builds peace and harmony, what makes for beauty and sublimeness. Truth is something we must work for, and work together for. The opposite of truth is error, and error leads to the death of beauty, and, ultimately, the state of war. But the problem with error is that, unlike mathematical error, which is simply incorrect, soul error—disruption or discord in the unison of inward sensibility and sensitivity—entangles the soul in such a way that one's inner sensibility and sensitivity is rendered immune to the fact. So we persist in our indigence, or, in religious language, our "sin," a term which in Greek literally means "missing the mark." Truth is the constructiveness which "hits the mark."

Truth happens, then, as part of a process or development, if it happens at all. The end is peace and harmony. The starting point at the social level is polite conversation and good manners, and, on the basis of this, real virtue is built up which becomes the truth of a life. If truth is constructive, two forces of the soul underlie it: renunciation and striving. The first of these is at the heart of *Journeyman Years*; the second, of *Faust*.

15. Goethe, *Journeyman Years*, 101.
16. Ibid., 245.
17. Ibid., 103.
18. Ibid., 203-4.
19. Ibid., 205.
20. Ibid., 286f.
21. Ibid., 159.

13

The Devil's Work

The Devil's work, so they say, is never done. That work is always soul-destroying. Goethe's *Faust* is published as "a tragedy in two parts"; it is an epic; it is also a dramatic exposé of modernity and its discontents. At the core of modernity and its discontents, *Faust* has it, is a wager with the Devil. This is the wager in the epic that Faust makes with Mephistopheles. But, quite strikingly, this wager is a symbol of modernity—and post-modernity no less. On one side, *Faust* may be read, without "reading in" to it too much, as a critique of modernity; and, on the other side, as about the possibility and impossibility of enchantment. The tragedy is that the possibility becomes increasingly impossible for Faust—and for modernity. History bears out Goethe's *Faust* myth. The book is more relevant and true now than when Goethe wrote it. We shall not understand modernity and its discontents if we do not understand *Faust*. The importance of closely reading this work (and I do not necessarily mean reading it with specialist expertise) can scarcely be over-emphasized. *Faust* is a foundational text of all humanistic culture—particularly Goethe's own brand of futuristic humanism, as I called it in the last chapter.

The two parts of *Faust* took Goethe over 60 years to write. Part One was published in 1808 (although there were earlier versions) and Part Two was published in 1832. Of course, the work is well known and everywhere regarded as a capital text of world literature. However, it is as difficult to interpret as the Bible; one could say it is endlessly interpretable. Not because it is so obscure that it could mean anything, but because it is so rich. As I said, we are interpreting *Faust* as being about the possibility of enchantment, and, of course, about the corresponding impossibility, tied up with the Faustian pact.

If we take *Faust* along (as we are) with the Wilhelm Meister novels, we can rightly assert I think that Goethe is the most important and authoritative writer on our subject, in the serious sense that we have meant this word all along as indicative of "metaphysical experience" and even the possibility of metaphysical experience, given our "new priority" we spoke of. What ties *Faust* together with the Wilhelm Meister novels, so different as they are from each other, is precisely *enchantment*. Faust goes more deeply into its *logic*.

Faust has the potential to magnify our discussion of enchantment so greatly, and to take it in so many directions, because the work is immensely porous—with philosophy, religion, literature, ethics, and politics all flowing through it, and being transformed by it—that the word "enchantment" suddenly seems too weak and vulnerable. Even so, to my mind, and insofar as I can tell, *Faust* has been repeatedly misunderstood; for anything to do with "enchantment" seems to get overlooked. There are all sorts of interpretations of *Faust*, even outright rejections of it as being unreadable,[1] but *Faust* as being about the work of enchantment is never taken seriously.

I will show clearly and easily what I believe: that enchantment is fundamental to both parts of *Faust*, although they are very different from each other. At the same time this will provide an elementary introduction to a complex but literally wonderful work. In a nutshell, *Faust* is a text about the life of the soul. It is not essentially religious in any pre-ordained sense, nor, even less, is it nonreligious. It is philosophical in approaching the life of the soul through the wisdom of love, but it almost takes a reverse approach so that the reader sees the truth by being shown folly and her brother hubris in their Sunday best and looking awfully impressive. The "reverse psychology" of *Faust* is part of the irony and indirectness by which Goethe gets behind all façades that masquerade as truth and understanding with regard to what is human and divine in a post-theological world, a world where theological language is basically defunct, as it was for Goethe, who only ever uses theological language to "misuse" it in its "proper" ecclesiastically defined didactic and dogmatic sense. *Faust* does not blind us by the light; it invites us into the darkness, all the better to attract us to the light in the same way that winter nights which draw in early and stay dark till late in the morning make us yearn for spring mornings and summer nights.

Faust is a work of art which, if it is read as being about the life of the soul, actually has the effect of *attuning* the soul somehow—or re-attuning it. Poetry has this power, and many poems—Rilke's, for example—have this power on our inner sensitivity and sensibility, but not in such an all-engaging sense as is given us by *Faust*, which, if anything, is not just to do with our personal attunement but the attunement of society and culture. In this, *Faust* stands unique, in a class of its own. The problem is that it is difficult and we need some keys to it if it is to work its magic.

At the beginning of Part One of *Faust*, Faust is completely disenchanted with life. He is unusually successful and well-off. His educational level is exceptional. And yet, he is jaded.

> I've studied now Philosophy
> And Jurisprudence, Medicine,—
> And even, alas! Theology,—
> And from end to end, with labour keen;
> And here, poor fool! With all my lore
> I stand no wiser than before... (I.1.1-6)[2]

The imagined setting is Gothic. In Scene Three, Mephistopheles appears to Faust in his chamber looking like a wandering scholar of the Middle Ages. Mephistopheles identifies himself: "I am the Spirit that Denies!" (I.3.161) And adds: "Thus all which you as sin have rated,—Destruction,—aught with evil blent,—That is my proper element." (I.3.165-7) Mephistopheles offers Faust his services that might afford him recreation (I.3.53f.). In Scene Four, Faust and Mephistopheles commit themselves to a pact. Mephistopheles says he can reveal life to him at last, and set him free from his tedium and listlessness (I.4.14). The pact takes shape in the course of a conversation in which Faust is by no means duped. It is in fact Faust himself who decides the main terms of the pact, that whatever pleasure he gets with Mephistopheles' help, he should never rest content with it, and if he does, then he will die (I.4.163-77).

Faust Part One is the tragedy of a person who believes it is possible to gain more than relief from *tedium vitae*: to gain enchantment, but on the basis of a wager.

According to the terms of the pact the enchanted moment is impossible, for Faust is bound to live for the next moment, and the next. Perhaps Faust imagines that, by desiring this, he will be accumulating all the experience of everything pleasurable that Mephistopheles has to offer him. Or perhaps Faust is gambling on dispelling his ennui by becoming a slave to unending desire. Faust's desire will not let the fruit rot on the vine; the fruit will always only be there just for the picking. Or perhaps, more metaphysically (after all, Faust is a philosopher and a theologian), Faust is uniting desire with time itself. The fleeting moments of time will become fleeting moments of desire, and vice versa. In this way for Faust, rather than time dragging, with moments seeming to "last forever" so that they become boring, he will always desire time and always have time for his desire. In this way his desire becomes as endless as time and, in a way, then, timeless. "Then Time be finished unto me!" Faust declares at the end of his statement to Mephistopheles (I.4.177). "Plunge me in Time's tumultuous dance, In the rush and roll of circumstance!" (I.4.225-6) Faust is aware that in plumbing the mysteries of time and desire, there will be distress and worry along with delight and success, but he concludes, "Restless activity proves the man!" (I.4.230)

They write the pact on paper and Faust signs it in blood. Mephistopheles is rather amazed at Faust's wherewithal. "Fate such a bold untrammelled spirit gave him, As forwards, onwards ever must endure; Whose over-hasty impulse drave him Past earthly joys he might secure." (I.4.327-30)

Scene Five takes place in a wine cellar, where Mephistopheles, unwittingly (it would seem, from the text) imitating Jesus' first miracle in John's Gospel, at the wedding feast at Cana, where the wine did not run out, gives it a twist of his own: any wine they spill turns to fire. Of course, wine is spilt in due course and the maddened drinkers chase Mephistopheles and Faust out of the tavern.

And so the whole of Part One is comprised of the adventures of Mephistopheles and Faust as the latter chases his desire of the moment for sensual pleasure and the former helps to make it possible.

The center of the action revolves around the beautiful girl, Margaret (or Gretchen, as she is always referred to). She is a sweet and lovely, innocent girl that Faust lusts after. To love her would be death for Faust as he would have to declare a moment sacred and want to stop time; but that is what he is not permitted to do by the terms of the pact that he has made. He desires to love her but cannot afford to do so and his lust for her and its success leads to her public shaming and moral destruction, the murder of her beloved brother who tries to interfere and, finally, her imprisonment.

Gretchen loves Faust truly but he cannot stay with her even while he seeks to rescue her at the end of Part One. The wager, it seems, can get him everything and nothing. That's the irony.

It is in a drug-fuelled moment that Faust first sees and "falls" for Gretchen. The "madness" or sorry infatuation follows and one can probably draw a straight line of logic between the first moment and the last, when she is condemned and in prison. As is often the case in society today, where a similar Faustian morality is called "individual freedom," and the victim and their family suffer forever while the perpetrator flies free or "gets off lightly," justice can hardly be said to prevail.

Faust's pact with Mephistopheles, the diabolical facilitator of Faust's wishes, binds him to the power of the now. Duration means death. Anything "lasting," then, is impossible. However, duration in time, time-honored-ness and what lasts are criteria of enchantment. Faust's pact ties him unwittingly to endless progress and development—but toward what? The mystique of progress and development are still today the watchwords of monetary economics, social policymaking, and liberal-democratic politics. The ends to which we are actually developing are never part of the discussion; it is simply assumed that this or that is a "development" and that is good enough. But a development is never a development if we do not know our destination. The Faustian pact, then, is implicitly critical of the Enlightenment myth: that humankind will continue to develop its knowledge as far as it can in a way which will be beneficial to all.

A society and culture bound to development will succeed in killing the thing it loves. This is not a paradox: it is an irony.

The power of educated reason to get what it wants by "free" means is not world-shaping, but, in the end, destructive. Individualism leads to the destruction of the individual.

The thesis of Adorno and Horkheimer's *The Dialectic of Enlightenment* (1949) is that Enlightenment reason extends the reign of reason everywhere to such an extent that the world becomes unreasonable. At an everyday level we experience this when we complain about bureaucracy and "red tape" or all the forms we need to fill out for the simplest thing. Historically (but also logically) it was a short road between the proclamation of freedom, fraternity, and equality in France in 1789 and the Reign of Terror in 1793-94. The culture of invincible progress and the science of the Enlightenment led not to universal peace and happiness, but to Auschwitz. For Adorno, there is an inevitability about the "dialectic of enlightenment" which people do not see, or do not want to see. But Goethe was probably among the first to see it and his vision remains the clearest.

Secularism and rationalism do the Devil's work, turning secularization (a good thing) into an ideology, an "ism," and turning reasonableness—in other words, what is most human—into a mental method. Secularity is deadened in secularism, as reason is deadened in rationalism. This is not a paradox either: it is an irony.

The wager can get Faust everything and nothing. It can get him everything he wants but not the one thing every person (if they are to be a person in a "full" and "meaningful" sense) must have: enchantment. And of course this includes, centrally, loving and being loved, as we have seen from Wilhelm Meister. And so *Faust* is a tragedy. The tragedy is that we wager on enchantment, in one way or another; but enchantment is exactly what we cannot achieve.

Enchantment, like love, of which it is a part, is outside any calculation.

Faust is a critique of our world, where it is believed money talks, and money makes the world go round, and the acquisition of money is the key to experience and the key to experience is the acquisition of money. In other words, *Faust* is a critique of the idea that we can get what we want through calculated means. Rather than loving and being loved, through calculation we destroy love and then go on (if we have the power) to destroy the world. Yet as we continue on our path of regrettable destruction, we will continue to fool ourselves that we have the key to success, to achievement, in our hand. But money dispels enchantment and love. All that is unconditional cannot be had for a wager. What is enchanting cannot be gambled upon. *Faust* Part One reveals this much at least.

Everything glamorous is a façade. All hubris is a lie. Both are life- and soul-destroying.

Faust gambles that enchantment can be had by experience and the accumulation of experiences and the power of now. But the accumulation of experiences and the power of now are inimical to enchantment. They are the way of conceited egotism. Reading, listening, and gazing are the way of enchantment and they each take *time*. For them *duration* is essential. Duration is what Faust gambles upon being irrelevant (like imagining; therefore tradition is irrelevant, when, in fact, it is most necessary that it be honored). All I need, Faust wagers, is to be in the now; the fullness of the moment is life. As he finds out, it is illusion and, ultimately, solitary confinement. The power of now as a "releasement" (*Gelassenheit*) of the past and the future leave one not with the fullness and plenitude of the enchanted moment but with vacuity. It is the eastern philosophy of nothingness, of Hindu, Buddhist, and western New Age styles of meditation, for example, that teach the reality of the moment and living for the moment alone. The tragedy is that this leads not to life but rather to death, for such a life extinguishes relationships which rely on duration, durability, longevity, vintage, wisdom of hindsight, patience, longsuffering, melancholy, and continued desire, all of which, among other things, comprise love.

Desire wants to perpetuate itself and *last*. Lasting desire is a satisfaction. *Eros* is not lusty desire as in our sex-fetish culture; *eros* is ground-breaking. *Eros* is ground-breaking desire because (as the words suggest) it *breaks new ground*. *Eros* is intense and durable. With these qualities not only can *eros* break ground, it can *provide* ground, and culturally, it does just that. When Marcuse wrote a book entitled *Eros and Civilization* (1955) it was not implausible, as it may at first have seemed, to think about these two concepts together and in terms of each other. For Marcuse, as for Freud, upon whom he was drawing for inspiration, "*eros*" signifies the inner aspect of life, here in its collective form, and "civilization" refers to the outward manifestation of what started within. In time, civilization shapes *eros*. Freud believed there was a potentially fatal mismatch between *eros* and civilization, and Marcuse further develops this view in his work. *Faust* is already cognizant of this mismatch; that is why it is a *tragedy*. The character of Faust trashes all stability and civilization to live for the moment. But he develops. His notion of the moment develops into a search for the eternal moment, which would not be a moment that "lasts forever," but the moment in which a life finds completion and its own finitude, in which, with Keats one might say: "now more than ever seems it rich to die/ To cease on the midnight with no pain." This moment would be one in which all is rectified and put right; like the Pauline concepts of justification and reconciliation. Faust, the tragedian, seeks an end to tragedy, and, of course, as it develops, this is not for himself but for his people, which, as a politician, he leads and represents; of course this people is a figure of humanity. This sought-for moment is the ultimate *enchanted moment*, a moment of eros and civilization in the ascendant, the true "power of now" as not just about me, but about all living creatures.

Faust Part Two is much longer and more difficult to read than Part One. The setting is neither "this" world, nor the "next" world, in the sense given by conventional theology; it is somewhere "unconscious," like a dream space. Therefore, anything can happen at any *moment*, and anyone can appear at any *time*. It is as if the *soul itself* were the setting: the inner sensibility and sensitivity given by culture and world literature. Such a soul could only be Goethe's and this is why *Faust* Part Two is his most personal work. It is psycho-autobiography. It is a primary text of the literature of enchantment.

What is being pursued across the dreamscape of *Faust* Part Two is redemption beyond the pact with Mephistopheles. Is Faust doomed by the pact, or can he, despite the pact, be redeemed? This is not just a question Faust might ask himself, but it is a question that faces a Faustian society, a Faustian *modernity*; and this is why *Faust* is relevant for study in the humanities today. The question still faces us and indeed it is becoming more crucial as time goes on.

There is a lot of recapitulation of Part One in Part Two. But before we look more at Part Two, we see that, at the end of Part One, Faust and Mephistopheles reconvene. This is the section entitled "Dreary Day" (I.23) and is set in a field. Faust does not rue the day he made the pact, but his disenchantment has become acute. The cost of being "absolutely modern" (to use the poet Rimbaud's apt expression), the cost of being always, in our way of thinking, after "the next best thing" is such that, to Mephistopheles, Faust is driven to say: "Murder and death of a world upon thee, monster!" (I.23.60-1) Yes, but the pain is that he is in thrall to this monster. And, by extrapolation, modernity—big capitalism—is in thrall to forces outside its control; it is forced to globalize, for instance, to impose the reign of commodification far and wide in order to keep profiting and developing. Like Faust, we can see the poverty we impose on whole continents as they are forced to be "the workshop of the world" and do what we can no longer afford to do, while we reassure our bad consciences that our business is lifting them out of poverty. Faust's ambivalence about the pact with Mephistopheles is ours, after Auschwitz.

Just after the start of Part Two we find Faust and Mephistopheles in "a gloomy gallery" (II.1.5).[3] The previous scene had been a pleasure garden and the Emperor's court, the glamour world and the world of pomp and circumstance, all rolled into one. In this recapitulation Faust says, "In our old days the fun of it/ Didst thou wear out, and I'll have none of it." (II.1.5.5-6) There is no going back for Faust. (Or for modernity: it has to go forward, like it or not.) Faust is not seeking to go back; he is faced with the problem of how to obey the Emperor's command that "he will instantly/ Helena and Paris before him see." (II.1.5.11-12) Paris and Helena are man and woman in all their beauty. They are also personifications of the classical world and the classical ideal. The Emperor wants them here, now. Part of the symbolism therefore has to do with marrying the classical and modern moments in a new culture beyond the Faustian "dialectic of Enlightenment," where reason is coupled to unreason. The point we want to notice is that disenchantment is at a new pitch, but the pact is not abandoned. In Part Two, Faust will seek redemption in the terms given by the pact at the beginning of Part One. In terms of society and culture, this must mean that *modernity is the key* to the answer to its problems. *Faust* would seem to be a work pitched to the other side of modernity and to the redemption of culture after the illusion of Enlightenment wears off, as it has done, I think, in our time.

Mephistopheles gives Faust a key to "the deepest depths" (II.1.5.47), where he is invited to "delve," there to find the Mothers. These are "Goddesses, unknown to ye,/ The Mortals,—named by us unwillingly." (II.1.5.45-6) Where are the depths, or where is the way to them? Faust enquires. "No way!" Mephistopheles exclaims, "To the unreachable—/ Ne'er to be trodden! A way to the Unbeseechable,/ Never to be besought! Art thou so prepared?" The image or idea of the Mothers chills Faust's blood; nevertheless, he is up for it: "Come on then! we'll explore, whate'er befall;/ In this, thy Nothing, may I find my All!" (II.1.5.83-4) If Faust can get to the deepest depths, where the Mothers dwell, with this key, he will find a tripod at "the utterly deepest bottom" (II.1.5.112). With the Tripod he will be able to conjure up Helena and Paris into actuality for the Emperor. The meaning of the Mothers, according to Goethe, is his own; he borrowed the reference from Plutarch. Without reading too much into it, which is easy enough to do, Faust is invited within this dream space—which is neither heaven nor earth, but an imaginative space in between, perhaps a connecting space—to descend. "Descend" here means the same as "ascend" in any case (II.1.5.103). Faust must deepen his soul into its unconscious and so he vanishes from view.

Our human tendency is not to wonder about the psychology of our depths, unless something bad happens to us and we realize our vulnerability, our fragility and the games we are caught up in playing:

The chill of dread is man's best quality. (II.1.5.100)

Dread moves humankind from torpor, stasis, rigidity, game-playing—and from the ritual, convention, and cyclical time (calendrical time or liturgical time, which always come back to where it started) that is part and parcel of living in a rut of disenchantment.

Faust's words would seem to indicate ways that we keep dread at bay and cordon off our lives from it. But there is no true Mystery without fear and trembling. This is very much the case in the Bible, of which Goethe had an intimate knowledge.

Faust succeeds in bringing Helena back to life. But her beauty proves too much for him:

> Have I still eyes? Deep in my being springs
> The fount of Beauty, in a torrent pouring! (II.1.7.111–12)

He collapses, perhaps fatally.

The beginning of Act Two recapitulates the scene in Faust's study from Part One. The room is unchanged, Faust lies unconscious on the bed and Mephistopheles is looking over him. Yet, we feel the distance in time between the occasion in Part One when Faust could receive Mephistopheles, and now, when he cannot any longer. Then, Faust had an inconceivably bright future; now, he needs time to recover. Then, he destroyed others; now he has almost destroyed himself. But the stakes are much higher. No longer is it Gretchen that he is smitten with, but the ideal beauty herself, Helena. No one had noticed Gretchen before Faust had; while the beauty of Helena is legendary and eternal. To embrace Helena, to love and be loved by her, would be to grasp the eternal moment. If Faust could just be in that moment, he would willingly break his pact and die in and for *that moment*. The shift between Part One and Part Two is from physical to metaphysical beauty.

The shift indicates that metaphysical experience and all striving, all desire therefore, has divine aspirations. Beauty, goodness, and truth seem to show the possibility of being *with* God or *like* God. But beauty comes upon us and smites us and sets the terms for what is good and true, and these are not logical but imperious. Overall, *Faust* is about these aspirations and this striving and the destruction they entail. And it is about the possibility of redemption, which means moving beyond the shadow will of Mephistopheles which accompanies Faust's every desire.

The social implications run parallel. Can modernity with its Faustian character move beyond the "negative dialectic," whereby every theory, every standpoint undermines itself and within which the identity of "the human" and "the divine" are theoretically undecidable? One of the reasons they are undecidable is that, in Adorno's words, "No theory today escapes the marketplace." He continues: "Each one is offered as a possibility among competing opinions; all are put up for choice; all are swallowed. There are no blinders for thought to don against this, and the self-righteous conviction that my own theory is spared that fate will surely degenerate into self-advertising."[4] Although this is a depressing prospect, social critical theory starts right here, and, as we saw right at the start of the book, so does any account of enchantment.

What happens is that Faust, through his striving, brings Helena back again. And this time he is not destroyed but able to unite with her; they have a son, Euphorion. Faust's ability to call up the Mothers proves his making, as the Homunculus says: "Who to the Mothers found his way/ Has nothing more to undergo." (II.2.3[1].56–7) But "bliss and beauty ne'er enduringly unite" (II.3.1450) and Faust loses both Euphorion and Helena toward the end of Act Three. Meanwhile, as Faust has been ascending, earlier on in Act Three Mephistopheles has been finding his element with "the Ugly." Faust continues to create himself anew and, as he does, Mephistopheles becomes disoriented and uncertain of himself and loosens or loses his power over Faust.

With this sketchy commentary, we should keep in mind that *Faust Part Two* is more than the story: the writing overflows the story on every side. There is a quite bewildering array of voices and the dreamlike quality of it all persists and gets ever stranger. The symbolism is suggestive, surreal, and manifold. The writing almost takes on the abstract quality of music, as if, rather than have us "understand" the story, we are purely to sense it in the qualitative way that musical notes come to our ears. But the characters and dialogue of Faust and Mephistopheles remain definite and provide continuity, so that, as in a dream, or a musical score, while we do not know what is next, we will not get lost.

The source of Faust's experience in Part One is desire; but desire takes him beyond love in the romantic sense to Helena, who represents the beauty that attracts him and which transcends him. But at the same time, Faust continues to glimpse Gretchen, for instance, at the beginning of Act Four, entitled "High Mountains," where he has been borne by cloud to Germany. The cloud takes a "godlike woman-form" (II.4.1.11) and seems like Juno, Leda, or Helena; and his first love Gretchen almost takes shape within his heart. At the end of Part Two, Gretchen will reappear in heaven to lead Faust on.

Faust becomes involved with the Emperor concerning government and the commonwealth. Mephistopheles tries to distract him, but with less and less success. His hold over Faust is slipping. In Act Five there is a jump in time and Faust is much older. He has roots in the kingdom and has earned a reputation by reclaiming land from the sea for the people. Mephistopheles tricks Faust into misusing his power, but Faust curses him for it. *Faust's striving* has brought him clear of Mephistopheles' power over him, yet he has not overcome evil with violence but with striving after his desire for higher things.

Again the social implications run parallel. It will be from the ceaseless striving of modernity that we will find the key which will take us beyond it. A Faustian society is one that is hell-bent on development and personal experience. In the story, this leads to destruction rather than the happiness of the multitude. Society must repudiate—as Faust eventually did—all that Mephistopheles represents. It is the vision of beauty, the source of enchantment, that enables Faust to do this, though not directly. The vision of beauty, even the union with beauty (with Helena, resulting in the only beloved son, Euphorion), keeps Faust striving but it also raises the level of the striving and desire. At the end of the story Faust will look upon the generations who will benefit from his work in future:

> And such a throng I fain would see, -
> Stand on free soil among a people free!
> Then dared I hail the Moment fleeing:
> "Ah, still delay—thou art so fair!"
> The traces cannot, of mine earthly being,
> In aeons perish,—they are there!
> In proud fore-feeling of such lofty bliss,
> I now enjoy the highest Moment,—this! (II.5.6.68–76)

The pact is concluded. Faust has kept it. He has discovered a moment that he would wish to keep. It is a moment of life's utmost responsibility, a moment in which one may legitimately talk of the beneficent heritage of responsibility—or the wisdom of love. This is more than an enchanted moment: it is the moment to end all moments; hence it is the moment of death too. This moment that Faust chooses to conclude his pact is a moment free from the negative energy of Mephistopheles. It is a moment of accomplishment. It is a moment "after the war" and such a moment, we detect, is always a moment of "reclamation." Culture after modernity is—if we may interpret Faust this graphically—a culture of reclamation. This is a culture of a "homeland"—but not in a nationalist sense, because the word indicates peacetime dwelling together; and not striving, but *being*; "A land like Paradise here, round about:/ Up to the brink the tide may roar without." (II.5.6.59-60) It is the old idea of the Promised Land, or the land of enchantment of fairytales. It is not a "global" culture, but an oasis that stands strong—more like Switzerland, then, if we are to think of the map of Europe. In the moment when he gazes on such a vision, Faust calls time to stop and he dies.

This is not the end of *Faust*, however. *Faust* depicts *the unity of life and death* beyond the striving, the competition, the greed, faith and fear of worldly interests, the pleasure-seeking and the lotus-eating that exist under so many different glamorous names; Faust found that none of this is enchanting. He found at last, almost by chance, unforeseen, coming "out of the blue," the enchanted moment when he had achieved something in this life *for posterity*, and he did so in a way that took responsibility, not just for himself, but for others, as far as the eye could see (as he looked out over his reclaimed land). The "Faustian moment" of enchantment is contrary to the Faustian pact in every respect. In the pact, Faust dies, but in the Faustian moment—or the time which Faust enters through the opening of that moment before his wondering gaze—Faust lives, and it seems he will live forever, not only in posterity and memory, but in the discovery that *there is no death*. There is only a beyond, like a dream of heaven, which the righteous will enter, if they can discover it. So enchantment in *Faust* is linked to the immortality of the soul, just as in the death of Bergotte in Proust and the Rilke of the Elegies.

The famous last lines of *Faust*, the most famous that Goethe wrote, read:

Das Ewig-Weibliche Zieht uns hinan.
The Woman-Soul leadeth us
Upward and on! (II.5.7.267–8).

The words (as, of course, for of all Goethe's words) are variously translated. The new Oxford translation has, "Eternal Womanhood/ Draws us on high."[5] I have often seen, when these lines are quoted out of context, the subject given as "the eternal feminine" as that which draws us on or up.

Let us first set aside some fallacies about the eternal feminine. This "Woman-Soul" is not a "principle" here in the sense of St Paul's "principalities and powers,"[6] which indicate metaphysical theological beliefs, sometimes in personified form as angels and demons, sometimes in abstract intellectual form, such as principles of "simplicity," "infinity," "immensity" and "eternity" ascribed to God, and so on. We should not imagine that the "eternal feminine" is a female godhead—though *she is* the ideal counterpart to Mephistopheles.

The eternal feminine *personifies that which is enchanting; that is to say she is the creator, preserver, and destroyer of enchantment*. This, I think, is the crux. Every religion knows some facet of her; some religions deny these facets and suppress them. In Keats' words in *Ode on a Grecian Urn*, the eternal feminine is the truth that is beauty, the beauty that is truth.

The "us" of the last lines, the "we" who are being drawn on as by the eternal feminine, are those of us who are reading, listening, and gazing; for this is the work of enchantment that *resists* the wiles and wonders of Mephistopheles and *beholds* the feminine.

"The feminine" is *in us*. Exoterically conceived, the feminine may be represented by the beautiful woman with her softness and limpid grace; or the one who draws men to war, as Helen did; or draws them to market, to do business, to gain prestige and power. The feminine is *in us* as the strength of weakness, of water stronger than rock, as spirit of life.

> The valley spirit dies not, aye the same;
> The female mystery thus do we name.
> Its gate, from which at first they issued forth,
> Is called the root from which grew heaven and earth.
> Long and unbroken does its power remain,
> Used gently, and without the touch of pain.[7]

The connotations of the last line of *Faust* lead us, as Goethe did, to think beyond patriarchal montheism and its theology. Goethe arrives at intuitions well known in Taoism. This verse from the *Tao Te Ching* famously describes the esoteric feminine. This is the eternal feminine that draws us on and that stands against Faustian culture that is ceaselessly in search of knowledge and experience and mistakes these for life—but mythologically the tree of life is another tree. In finding that moment of freedom, which is not knowledge, it is Mephistopheles and his counterparts that stop us dead in our tracks, and the eternal feminine, the "valley spirit" that draws us on.

Faust is itself erotic, imbued with feminine nature, because to understand its message of enchantment we must be *seduced*. Goethe provides an alternative myth for culture to guide institutions and individuals. It is one of the most extraordinary achievements in all literature. Goethe intends to seduce us and to seduce modern culture away from Faustian culture. It is a revolutionary text from a revolutionary time for a possible future. But without proper learning in the humanities, and with the totalizing reign of a Mephistophelian modernism given to striving, competition, development, progress, and the globalization of capitalist commercialization, our culture becomes deadened, and Goethe's great work falls on people who have deaf ears and who are barely able to read in that contemplative sense necessary for seduction and the soul-work of the valley spirit. Immanently speaking—and practically—what this means is the cultivation of a gentle presence. Reading, listening, and gazing call for and command a gentle presence.

There is triumph beyond the tragedy in *Faust*. After the breaking of the pact with Mephistopheles and Mephistopheles' falling away into Nothingness, saying, "I'd rather choose the Void forever," (II.5.6.93) that triumph is the redeeming grace of beauty that Faust goes on to experience. Beauty in Goethe remains, then, beyond "truth," our hope. While beauty captivates us, we cannot capture it; even art only pays tribute; beauty always deigns, as it were, to come to us; the work of enchantment provides the conditions by which this may happen and a suitable conduit for *Eros*.

Notes

1. William Frederic Hauhart, *The Reception of Goethe's Faust in England in the First Half of the Nineteenth Century* (1909) (Montana: Kessinger, 2008), esp. Chaps. 2 and 3.
2. All cited passages, unless otherwise indicated, come from Goethe, *Faust. A Tragedy in Two Parts*, trans. Bayard Taylor, 1870–71 (Oxford: Oxford University, 1952).
3. While the references to Part One read *Part: Scene: Lines*; the references to Part Two read *Part: Act: Scene: Lines*. The current reference therefore refers to Part Two, Act One, Scene Five.
4. Adorno, *Negative Dialectics*, 4.
5. Goethe, *Faust*, trans. David Luke (Oxford: Oxford World Classics, 2008), 239.
6. Cf. Romans 8:38; Colossians 1:16; Ephesians 6:12.
7. Lao-tzu, *Tao Te Ching*, trans. J. Legge, *Sacred Books of the East*, vol. 39 (Oxford: Clarendon Press, 1891), 75. I leave this verse for the poetic intuition of my reader. However, the commentary adds: "The spirit of the valley" has come to be a name for the activity of the Tao in all the realm of its operation [i.e. "heaven and earth"]. "The female mystery" is the Tao with a name of Chapter 1, which is "the Mother of All Things"; the Tao conceived without a name is "the Originator of heaven and earth."

14

The Joy of Enchantment

The time has come to look back at all that we have explored and review the signal stages along the way. The book has not been a theory of enchantment, nor have I attempted to theorize enchantment, either in itself or in terms of any other "discipline." I have not wanted to discipline this thing, enchantment, which is free.

At the beginning, we mapped out some preliminary, starting points. The first was to bring into view the importance of enchantment; the second, to see that enchantment is not the same at all times and in all places, and that it manifests historically, in time and place, as *cultural*. Culture has to do with how and why we cultivate ourselves personally and socially, and is a philosophical matter first and foremost. We looked at what saying that enchantment is cultural means for us now. It means, we said, a new priority, because disenchantment and the power of a socioeconomic system sustained by the Progress myth of the nineteenth century, which is pragmatic and utilitarian in ethos, can lead to only greater and greater disenchantment of the world, disenchantment in social relations, and disenchantment in our inner sensibility and sensitivity.

Our preliminary considerations set out, we turned then, in the bulk of the book, to Proust, Rilke, and Goethe, whose work we took, as one might take an icon, not in itself, but as pointing to something beyond itself that could be discerned through it. The lineaments of that which we wanted to discern was, of course, enchantment.

By increasing our sense of enchantment, we thought we might better understand that *work of enchantment* which it entailed. The case I wanted to make, and which I hope I have gone some way to making, is that, while the work of enchantment, reading, listening, and gazing, are outwardly passive and seemingly "useless" and "a waste of time" unless you can "spare the time" or have "time on your hands," inwardly, reading, listening, and gazing are potent activities, which, in our present state of culture, are neglected and virtually forgotten. We thought, too, that education without adequate practices of reading, listening, and gazing, such as we set out thanks to Proust and Rilke in the first instance, is no education at all. The demise of the proper practices of reading, listening, and gazing, as distinct from their pastiche versions, which are easily mistaken for our more serious considerations, go along with the demise of the humanities in education and in culture. This was not a theory on my part, to begin with anyway, but something we are alerted to by reading Proust and Rilke. The work of enchantment and enchantment itself are what the work of such great artists bring into view the way an icon for a believer brings into view the lineaments of the divine. This is the gift and power of art.

With Proust, we looked at the work of enchantment, reading, listening, and gazing, as values and as activities. With Rilke, we remarked on the erotic and narcissistic lineaments of enchantment and the work of enchantment that discerning these entails. In Goethe's work, in our final chapters, we looked at the social and temporal sides of the question. This is where the question of culture came up most notably. Goethe seems to provide, through his works, a critique of western culture as he saw it, which was as something ultimately self-destructive and continually widening its ambit of self-destruction—as something, in other words, dragging more and more of the world into its melee. Goethe did not see the remedy elsewhere, however, but as coming from within western culture, his culture, as an alternative reality. There is a quality about Goethe's writing that one can only call, *with* its religious connotations, "scriptural." Scriptures are of course revered writings, writings called "holy" because, as the word says, they "stand apart." The importance of reverence to enchantment, and to the alternative reality Goethe's long novels and his Faust tragedy put before us, is not the only thing clearly marked in his work, though, for so too is the due placement of reverence, without religiosity on one hand or superstition on the other.

Well, what does all this add up to? I cannot deny that it is hard to say. From the first, I have said that my work is suggestive, not prescriptive. I have also said, from the first, that my work is to be encouraging, by which I meant to tempt—even seduce—my reader into the work of enchantment because, ultimately, enchantment is not found in a book or anywhere else, but in the work, and the work must always *lead on*. To engage reading, listening, and gazing—to engage works of art and life—is the first and main thing to "conclude."

The work of enchantment, in the simplest sense of properly reading, listening, and gazing, has to do with engendering moments of enchantment, such as that described, famously, in Proust, where he dips his little piece of madeleine into lime-blossom tea that his Aunt Léonie has made for him after Mass one Sunday. This moment recalls for Proust a flood of recollections of his boyhood. The novel, whose title is poorly rendered as "In Search of Lost Time" in some current English translations, is not a search for lost time at all: *it is a recollection of enchanted time*. The recollection or remembrance, moreover, takes place *in time*. So right through Proust's novel, there is a *doubling* of time in the moment: then *and* now. This way time is more real, and life more realized, in the artistic sense of more perfect. Proust shows, right through his novels, as their mainstay in fact, that "then" enchants "now," when nothing much may be happening, and it does so because it is a contemplative moment. Time doubles in this way only in remembrance. But we who read Proust experience a simulation and imitation of the experience he describes in his novel, for the time that enchants his narrator enchants us his readers too, and we find our own experience of time double: the time *of* which we read and the time *in* which we read. Of course, this is the case with any novel, but its meaning in terms of enchantment is brought before us in Proust as it is nowhere else, for most writers are simply unconscious of the fact and ascribe little or no meaning to it at all. Proust extends our world of enchantment and his memories become ours, albeit imaginary ones.

The danger of this is that our memories may be bad and even traumatic and so we live haunted lives, like ghosts. Goethe is obviously aware of this danger, which can disrupt a society and culture at the level of its soul if something unwholesome or even evil is endemic to that society. There can be disturbed individuals and there can be disturbed sectors of society. This, I think, is why Goethe puts so much emphasis on education. For him, education has an almost salvific value and is the most futuristic enterprise a society can be bent upon. In a literate, civil society such as ours, only education can create the social conditions by which individuals may be born and have the kinds of memories Proust could recall. In other words, the remembrance of things past, as a work of enchantment, is not natural: it is cultural.

Faust shows us a humanitarian love when Faust beholds the peace he has achieved for his people, but he achieves this despite himself and, also, despite all that is Mephistophelean. On the way we see various kinds of love: romantic, domestic, and patrician. And we see disastrous love too, for instance, when sex is an object of it, as between Faust and Gretchen in Part One. The love Faust eventually finds at the end of Part Two is "not of this world" because it comes down from above, from beyond death. Mercy and forgiveness are preconditions of this love which is "true" in another sense than the true love I just referred to with respect to Proust. This love is an ultimate mystery of some kind. Once more Goethe supplements Kant. For this love is no longer in time or place such as we know and are familiar with, yet we may experience it. Gretchen, now dead, returns and says:

Incline, O Maiden,
With Mercy laden,
In light unfading,
Thy gracious contenance upon my bliss!
My loved, my lover,
His trial is over
In yonder world, returns to me in this! (II.5.7.226f.)

This love is beyond our avowedly twisted secular metaphysics, and is overtly religious in a sense understood in traditional Christianity.

Finally, I need to leave my reader with some insight into the phrase "the unity of life and death" that we have had to refer to in our pages; and I will do so now. I will illustrate it with a story, rather than prevaricate theoretically about what I do not know and cannot know.

The story is not mine, but that of Isaac Bashevis Singer, a Nobel-Prize-winning novelist who lived most of his life in New York. It is the story of the grief of Rabbi Bainish and is simply entitled "Joy" in the collection of short stories entitled *Gimpel the Fool* (1957). The story speaks of the unity of life and death and the moment of enchanted joy in which it is apparent. The story is set in central Europe before the Nazis and their accomplices wiped out the little Jewish villages there, where Hasidic culture had developed relatively educated, peaceful, and crime-free communities which were unique in the annals of humankind. It begins as follows: "Rabbi Bainish of Komarov, having buried Bunem, his third son, stopped praying for his ailing children. Only one son and two daughters remained, and all of them spat blood. His wife, frequently breaking into the solitude of his study, would scream, 'Why are you so silent?'"[1] She would berate him fiercely and at length, but he would reply, "Leave me alone!" "When Rebecca, his youngest, died, the rabbi did not even follow her hearse. He gave orders to his sexton Avigdor, to close the shutters, and they remained closed. Through a heart-shaped aperture in the shutters, came a meager light whereby the old rabbi looked through books." Actually the rabbi is only 50, but he has aged greatly and seems much older. Although he pretends to study, it is out of habit; he has lost his faith in God and this, for him, is a psychological torture to add to his other woes. A rabbi is no better than his following and Rabbi Bainish's following begin to desert him. Unable to bear her solitude, his wife leaves for an extended stay with her brother. The House of Prayer, a simple structure, normally the center of the little community's identity, begins to fall into disrepair. The idea of God, especially of a just God who is interested in humanity, the rabbi has come to believe is a mockery. The holy books of his community are all a lie. The rabbi no longer takes care of himself and gives all his possessions away. Life seems utterly pointless. One day, on the way to the community bathhouse, the rabbi idly picks a berry from a bush which he knows is poisonous and thinks: "If a thing like this can turn one into a corpse...If everything hinges on a berry, then all our affairs are berries." The rabbi continues to fast, in fact to starve himself, and with time he becomes painfully fragile looking.

As the rabbi sat half-awake, half slumbering in his old chair, his arms on the armrests, engrossed in thoughts he did not know he was thinking, divested of all external things, he suddenly caught sight of his youngest daughter, Rebecca. Through the closed door she had entered and stood there, erect, pale, her hair plaited in two tresses, wearing her best gold-embroidered dress, a prayer-book in one hand, a handkerchief in the other. Forgetting that she had died, the rabbi looked at her, half-surprised. "See, she's a grown girl, how come she's not a bride?" An extraordinary nobility spread over her features; she looked as though she had just recovered from an illness; the pearls of her necklace shone with an unearthly light, with the aura of the Days of Awe. With an expression of modesty and love she looked at the rabbi.

"Happy holiday, Father."

A brief conversation takes place and the daughter half-commands, half-implores the rabbi, her father, to join the others at the holiday meal. Suddenly the rabbi comes to his senses.

An icy shudder ran through the rabbi's spine. "But she's dead!" At once his eyes were drenched with tears, and he jumped to his feet as though to rush toward her. Through the mist of tears Rebecca's form became distorted, grew longer and partly blurred, but she still loomed before him. The rabbi noticed the silver clasp of her prayer-book and the lace of her handkerchief. Her left pigtail was tied with a white ribbon. But her face, as though veiled, dissolved into a blotch. The rabbi's voice broke.
"My daughter, are you here?"
"Yes, father."
"Why have you come?"

"For you."
"When?"
"After the holiday."

After the apparition, or whatever it was, the rabbi goes out and celebrates with the others. He seems charismatic in his fervor and his teaching has never seemed so inspired. Everyone is amazed at the sudden change in him. In the months that follow, with various other feasts, word about his miraculous recovery gets around, his followers return even with new followers joining them, his wife comes home. "On Hashanah Raba he prayed all through the night, until dawn, with his Hassidim. On Simchas Torah, he never wearied of dancing around the reading stand." But after the feast of Succoth he needs to lie down. "The moment he lay down he became moribund. His face grew as yellow as his fringed garment. His eyelids closed." He becomes altered. He would not let his wife call a doctor. His final words are, "One should always be joyous."

This story has the quality of a parable. It speaks the unity of life and death, perhaps in a way impossible for some of us to believe, although these things become easier to believe when one lives close up to them, not at a safe distance, untouched by the pain of loss (something hard to do in this world in any case). For Rilke, the unity of life and death had to do with living a death we can call our own as well as a life that we can call our own. He saw a time coming (our time) when it would be well nigh impossible to do either—our death would be stolen from us by the name of the disease attached to it and rather than seeing death as the brimming of life to the rim, we would regard it as a termination by the disease by which our death is labeled by the hospital system. But in his later work, in the final Elegy, for example, we are shown death more broadly as the side of life averted from us. In a letter written on the Feast of the Epiphany (January 6th) 1923 to Countess Margot Sizzo-Noris-Cruoy, one of his aristocratic confidantes, Rilke writes:

> It is conceivable that [death] stands infinitely closer to us than our effort would allow (this has grown ever clearer to me with the years, and my work has perhaps only the *one* meaning and mission to

bear witness, more and more impartially and independently—more prophetically perhaps, if that does not sound too arrogant—to this insight which so often unexpectedly overwhelms me)—our effort, I mean, can *only* go toward postulating the unity of life and death, so that it may gradually prove itself to us. Prejudiced as we are *against* death, we do not manage to release it from its misrepresentations—[2]

Rilke goes on to persuade the Countess that rather than being the "opposite" of life or "the negation" (dead abstractions in any case), death is "a *friend*, our deepest friend." Of course, Rilke did not mean the death one person inflicts upon another (in whatever name it is done), but what, 20 years previously, in the last part of *The Book of Hours* (1905) entitled, *The Book of Poverty and Death*, he had referred to as a death that is particular and suited to our life, a death that we can call our own. And then to the Countess: "Indeed, death (I adjure you to believe!) is the true yea-sayer. It says only: Yes. Before eternity."[3]

At the other end of life, from birth, as we grow up, we automatically know, as part of being aware, that we are not just "here" like a stone, but that we are positioned and, within that circumstance which is our life, we feel a sense of purpose and determination. Often, the arrival at this sense in a young person is called "the age of reason." This is why the death of any young person in any circumstances is so appalling. Not just that "someone has died" but that something is missing from the world as a result: someone who "should" be here is not. We may recall those lines of Proust I quoted earlier in this book:

> Certainly our experiments with spiritualism prove no more than the dogmas of religion that the soul survives death. All that we can say is that everything is arranged in this life as though we entered it carrying the burden of obligations contracted in a former life; there is no reason inherent in the conditions of life on this earth that can make us consider ourselves obliged to do good, to be fastidious, to be polite even, nor to make the talented artist consider himself obliged to begin over a score of times a piece of work.[4]

Art points to this unity of life beyond birth and death, to a unity in which there is no barrier and, if we are sufficiently distracted from the exigencies of the day-to-day, Rebecca may interrupt our musings and we may not notice the fact that she is dead. Art does not just point out this matter, but carries us *into* the experience of it *in* the experience of art, of reading, listening, and gazing. That is why these activities, which are commonly regarded as, if not a waste of time, something to do in your spare time, are in fact so absolutely important for every one of us. That is why education that does not have them at its heart is no education at all and, in fact, in our world, we do speak instead of "training," and education is little more than that now either at school or at university. This is more than a sorry fate for culture and civilization: it is a signal of demise.

Reading, listening, and gazing not only engender the experience of enchantment by means of preparing and readying us, but they are ways of *recuperating* the soul as well as, at the same time, disrupting the culture industries. By the "soul" I mean our capacity for soulfulness. Against this soulfulness is the crassness of commodity capitalism with all its primitive fetishism and "reification," as Adorno called it, by which he meant the production of the realisms and objectivisms that I quoted Levinas lamenting at the start of the book. Against this soulfulness as well is the soullessness of glamour, which, while it looks inviting, even irresistible on occasion, and is ever "useful," will never be soul-making. Reading, listening, and gazing, in the sense given to them in this book, give us *time* where striving and competition cease—although the Faustian world of striving and constant progress and "updating" is constantly bidding us to read, listen, and look, and so it can be confusing. If we only read, listen, and look in the Faustian sense, for example, by reading always "the latest," or looking at the television, or listening to "pop," we will never flourish, and enchantment will not be part of our world at all. The time of reading, listening, and gazing is an *inner* time. Enchantment is a soul-experience because it arises out of contemplative times.

Religion circumvents enchantment and the work of enchantment at its peril. Pomp tries to "stand in" its place and impress us, which it, of course, can easily do because it is in the nature of pomp to do so; at its best it is dazzling. But it can only supply a semblance of enchantment. A child who is easily enchanted will not even "get" the pomp and ceremony; we have to corrupt her nature somewhat first. Pomp is a pantomime version of enchantment for grown-ups. This comment is not to disparage the beauty of, say, a liturgy, done beautifully. Pomp looks beautiful but is "hollow"; that is the difference. Of course, a liturgy may be hollow too; it depends on whether it has soul or not. Liturgy without the work of enchantment will be merely ceremonialism. On the other hand, Puritanism tries to ignore enchantment. So you have placeless religion which is the same everywhere you go, and "timeless" religion which believes virtually the same all the time no matter what. In a word, you have ideology. If Catholicism is liable to suffer from the former, Protestantism is liable to suffer from the latter; but now that the two kinds of Christianity have become, over time, more akin, both can easily suffer from either. Even secular ideologues are "Puritans" in this sense of placeless and timeless beliefs; modern atheism is a prime example.

On the road to Damascus, Saul (the future St Paul) was blinded by the light. It was Christ risen from the dead who he could not see but could hear, although, in one of the accounts of the episode, those who were with Saul on the road could not hear the voice he heard. Now, Paul as we know has given the definitive interpretation of the person and work of Jesus, which, puzzlingly, he did without reference to any events in the life of Jesus before his death. But so authoritative is Paul's interpretation of Jesus that it comprises a significant portion of the New Testament, and his writings are therefore regarded as holy by Christians. However, Paul's (Saul's) moment of enlightenment on the road to Damascus, if we recall, does not circumvent the work of enchantment. What turns the Pharisee, Saul, into the Christian, Paul, is not the encounter on the road to Damascus, but the days that followed. Struck temporarily blind, Saul was taken into a friend's house, where he reflected on the Scriptures that he knew by heart, he listened to his friends and to his inner promptings, and he gazed into the darkness. In those days Saul engaged with the work of enchantment and it is only as a result of this work that the precious "encounter" that set it all off became a turning point. This is an example of the "spiritual" and the work of enchantment working together. We may often observe this in the life of saints. We may often observe it in reading the Bible. When Jesus says "Follow me" to Peter, Peter leaves his nets and follows Jesus, but if we read on in the Gospel, we realize that Peter is accused by Jesus of being Satan, in their little conversation in the district of Caesarea Philippi, and then later still Peter denies that he knows Jesus and is left feeling guilty of betrayal, especially since he had sworn to Jesus' face he would never betray him. Peter does not actually follow Jesus in any proper sense until the Pentecost after Jesus' death. It is then that he starts healing people and speaking with authority; it was the result of having contemplated many things and having been quite changed and inwardly enlarged as a result. His was the enchantment of a kind of love which was not homo-erotic, but was what the Greeks called *agape*, by which they meant *dispassionate* love, such as that of a god who lets it rain on the just and the unjust alike without distinction. *Agape* was interpreted early on as equivalent to the Latin *caritas* (charity) and came therefore to mean *compassionate* love, which today we might understand as "humanitarian" love. Following Jesus had to do with embracing humanity and a vision of peace, not traipsing round Galilee with him, but this conviction only came at a remove and it is precisely the "remove" that is important and where enchantment enters in.

> *There is no theory that is not a fragment,*
> *carefully prepared, of some autobiography.*
>
> —Paul Valéry

Notes

1. Isaac Bashevis Singer, "Joy," in *Gimpel the Fool* (1957) (Harmondsworth, Middlesex: Penguin Books, 1981), 107–16.
2. Rilke, *Letters 1910–1926*, trans. Jane Bannard Greene & M. D. Herter Norton (New York: Norton, 1969), 317.
3. Ibid.
4. Proust, *The Captive*, Part One, 250.

Index

Adorno, Theodor 27, 76, 115, 146
   Aesthetic Theory 12
   culture industry 13
   Dialectic of Enlightenment 140
   metaphysical experience 28
   names and 65
   Negative Dialectics 27, 145
   on Proust 35, 38, 56, 57
   twisted secular metaphysics 29
aesthetics 46
Agape 127, 163
America 110, 121, 123
angel 99, 100, 101, 107
anxiety 31
arcadia 68
art
   experience of 7, 28
   as gift 96, 97
   as heartwork 92
   as service to life 93
   turning 104
   and unity 161
Auschwitz 30, 44, 56, 63, 68, 140, 143
Austro-Hungarian Empire 89

Balzac, Honoré 47
beauty 145, 151
Beckett, Samuel 27
   Waiting for Godot 29
Berg, Alban 12
Bettelheim, Bruno 8
Bible 135, 145
Bourdieu, Pierre 14
Brontës, the 47
Buber, Martin 77

calculative thinking 5
capitalism 13, 58, 72, 90, 97, 109, 112, 116, 150
   commercialization 46, 85
   commodification 22, 110-111, 119-120
   globalization 24, 150
Celan, Paul 27
Cézanne, Paul 108
Chaplin, Charlie 15
charm 62, 71, 84
children 24
Christmas 108
Comte-Sponville, André 118
conversations 18
Cotswolds 68
culture 23, 25, 123, 125, 153
   after modernity 148
   Faustian 150
   humanistic 135
   knotting 130
   new 130

dark knowledge 86
de Certeau, Michel 119
death 61, 157ff., 106, 148, 156, 159, 160
depth 84, 91, 144, 148
descent 144
desire 141
Devil 135
Dickens, Charles 69
   Dickensian 69
disenchantment 5, 49, 51, 153
Disney 46
Dostoevsky 21

dread 144, 145
duration 141, 142
dying
   Albertine 52
   Bergotte 39-40
   how to 37, 148

Earth 128
Easter 112
Education 26, 104, 124, 154, 156
Elijah 45
Eliot, T.S. 79
   Ash Wednesday 1930 79
enchanters 83, 121
enchantment 24
   art and 4, 61
   culture and 2, 130-1, 153
   dark, as 92, 95ff.
   and the dead 98
   death and 61
   definition of 3, 57, 61
   development and 116
   enchainment as 89, 101
   Eros and 85, 141
   existence as 105
   experience of 1, 126
   falling into 44
   in *Faust* 136ff.
   as feminine/womanly 120, 121, 123, 149
   fiction and 69
   as frame 125-6
   indirect approach to 3
   as love 128
   melancholy and 78, 80, 98
   memory and 68-9
   the open and 100
   as power of now 142
   rallying cry to 46
   rapture as 86-7, 126
   realism and 123
   time as 115, 126, 141, 155
   transformation and 104, 109
   work and 103
   world as 126
enlightenment 162
ethics 107, 131, 150

faith 124
fame 72
Faust
   as critique of our world today 140-1
   Faustian 138-9
   modernity and 142
feminine 120, 149, 150
film industry 14
fin de siècle 58
Freud, Sigmund 17, 47, 77-8, 83, 85, 108, 142

gazing 7-8
gelassenheit 141
glamour 13
Glastonbury 69
God 125, 129
Goethe, Johann Wolfgang von 18, 155ff. 135ff.
   Apprenticeship 116ff.
   Bible and 145
   Conversations With German Refugees 118ff.
   Faust 135ff.
   Journeyman Years 116ff.
   the three reverences 124, 125, 128, 155
   Wilhelm Meister 115, 116ff.
goodness 145
ground-moods 79, 80

happiness 80
Hardy, Thomas 68
   The Woodlanders 68
hearing 55, 56
Hegel, G. W. F. 27, 38, 119
   Logic 57
Heidegger, Martin 38
highest reverence 124
Hiroshima 30-31, 32
Hölderlin, Friedrich, 97
Holocaust 21, 30, 101
holy 70
homeland 98, 148
Hook Norton 68
humanism 110, 124, 131, 135, 163
humanities 6, 23, 26, 59, 154

icons 8, 35, 75, 76, 116
inanimate nature 123
ineffability 47, 59
inner life 22

Jabès, Edmond 27
jargon 72
Jerusalem 65, 70
Jesus 44, 69, 107, 123, 163
Joseph of Arimathea 69
joy 102
jubilation 101, 105
justice 147

Kafka, Franz 7, 85
Kant, Immanuel 21, 29
Kat von D 15-16
Keats, John 78
 Ode on Melancholy 78, 142, 149
Kierkegaard, Søren 24
know thyself 12

lament 99
language 49
lesbianism 47
Levinas, Emmanuel 22, 26, 30, 31, 79
life-after-death 39-40
listening 7
living dead the 11
London 69
love 44, 122-3, 124, 127, 128, 141, 163
 expiring 47

Maimonides, Moses 3
Mallarmé, Stéphane 108
Mann, Thomas 17
manners 118
Marcel, Gabriel ix
Marcuse, Herbert 141-2
melancholy 78-9, 98
melody 55
mental illness 1
metaphysical experience 32, 36, 37, 38, 44, 45, 46, 51, 145
 angels and 101
 unity and 99
Michelangelo 96
Miller, Arthur 39

mind's eye 51
modernity 135ff. 143, 147
 as key to itself 144
 monstrous vanities 58
Moses 45
mourning 147-9
music 146
 transformation 59

Names
 fantasy unleashed and 64
 friendship and 72
 love and 71
 of places 63, 106
Nancy, Jean-Luc 7
Narcissus 84, 87, 93, 103
nature 123, 125
negative dialectic 145
New Age 8, 90, 130, 141
new priority 11, 21
news 119-120
Nietzsche, Friedrich 21, 75, 77, 97, 108,
 The Gay Science 77

open, the 100, 107
Orpheus 105
Orphism 107
Oxford 67

Paul, St. 142, 162
Perec, Georges 47
phenomenological method 8
philosophy 46
 blindness in 57
 feminine and 41, 149
pietism 16
Plato 27
poetry
 poetic thinking 17-18, 50
 as self-transformation 51
pomp 16, 163
post-Christian 21
posterity 148
post-modernity 32, 38
power of words 47
pragmatics 49, 57, 131
presence 72

progress 32
Propertius 76
Protagoras 125
Protestant ethic 4
Proust 4, 6, 35ff. 43ff. 55ff. 61ff. 108
   Captive, The 36
   Cities of the Plain 52
   Combray 63
   first love 70
   genius of 47
   Lost Time 36, 52, 63, 67, 155
   Remembrance of Things Past /
     In Search of Swann's Way 43
   versatility in depth 38
Psychoanalysis 49, 50
pure space 80
Puritanism 16, 163

reason 16, 143
recollection 155
Reé, Paul 77
renunciation 119, 121, 122
resemblances 44, 45, 132
resurrection 109, 112
reverence 124, 125, 155
   realized 128
reverse psychology 136
Rilke, Rainer Maria 75ff. 83ff. 95ff.
   103ff. 122, 137
   angels 87, 95
   Duino Elegies 76, 90, 95, 96
   Life of Mary 83
   Narcissus 83
   Notebook of Malte Laurids
     Brigge 86
   Sonnets to Orpheus 95, 103ff.
   The Turning 89, 90, 92
Rimbaud, Arthur 143
Ritualism 16
Rodin, Auguste 108
Ruskin, John 97
Russia 101

Salomé, Lou Andreas 51, 75,
   Die Erotik 77, 78, 85
   Memoir 87
Schopenhauer, Arthur 119
scientific thinking 17-18

scripture 154
secularity 140
Sermon on the Mount 39
sexuality 78-9, 84, 103, 156
Shaftesbury 69
Shakespeare, William 117
   Hamlet 117, 118
Singer, Isaac Bashevis 157
   Gimpel the Fool 157
social-critical theory 13, 46, 146
Soloviev, Vladimir 21
soul 23, 24, 25, 101, 102,
   open and 56
   reading and 98
   soul time 85
   unpicked 49
speculum 129
spirit 101, 106
spirituality 26, 83
striving 131, 145, 147

Tao 150
technology 22, 58
terroir 110
theatre 117
things 109-10, 111
time
   immeasurable 86
   soul and 85
   timebends 39
Tisbury 69
Tolstoy, Lev 76, 108
transfiguration 45
transubstantiation 45, 104, 105
Trollope, Anthony 69
truth 53, 132, 145

unity of experience 99
   of life after death 148, 156ff.
utilitarianism 4, 131
Uttley, Alison 68
   The Country Child 68

valley way of soul 150
Valéry, Paul 108
Varda, Agnes 13
Vermeer 37, 40

Wagner, Richard 77
Waits, Tom 15
war 89, 118
Weber, Max 4
Wessex 69
Westhoff, Clara 87
White, Jack 15
Wittgenstein, Ludwig 17
words 50
    enchantment of 50
    power of 52–3

Franklin Pierce University

00197168

DATE DUE

PRINTED IN U.S.A.